Divine Downloads

Find Your Real Identity

and Worth

LINDA LANGMAN

Divine Downloads

ISBN 9781097172528

Unless otherwise indicated, all scriptural quotations are from the King James Version of the Bible.

Cover Design by Karen-Marie Gariba
jubileekarenmarie@gmail.com

Editing and formatting by Doris Schuster, CES Publishing
www.ChristianEditingServices.org

DEDICATION

I dedicate this book first and foremost to the glory of
my Heavenly Father, Jesus my Lord and Friend, and
to the Holy Spirit, my Comforter and Helper.

To my loving husband, Dave. You are my treasure.

To my daughter Amy, my son-in-law Tim,
and my grandchildren, Cameron,
Jeffery, Donnick, Lucy and Jack.

You are such a joy in my life.

ACKNOWLEDGMENTS

Special thanks to Pastors Zak and Karen-Marie Gariba for believing in me and this project, and for your continual encouragement. Karen-Marie you went above and beyond to help me complete this assignment. You are a blessing. My deep appreciation to Doris Schuster for your friendship, support and your hard work on the manuscript. Thanks to all who prayed.

Table of Contents

Preface

How to use this book:
- as a personal daily devotional
- in a group study, choosing 2 to 3 subjects per week
- as a handy resource guide for topical study from
  the Table of Contents
- as a gift
- as a practical tool to share the good news with others

Divine Downloads are Bible truths from God to speak over yourself. As you read each devotional, ask God to make these truths come alive to you. Ask Him to partner with you to implement them into your life. Speak aloud the title and the confession at the end of each chapter as your personal declaration. Put them in your phone or on a card to speak throughout the day. "Camp" on the topics you struggle with until your mind is renewed and you "get it." You can also go to the Table of Contents page and speak aloud all of the titles. These truths will overpower any lies you have believed about yourself. You may want to highlight the Bible verses and speak those as well, for God's Word is living and powerful. Revelation of the power of your words and the authority of God's Word, mixed with your faith, is life-changing.

This book is not a one-time read. It is a manual for life. Keep it handy for quick reference to bring help and truth for everyday living. I, too, will be using it often to improve my Christian walk. This book will direct you to *the* Book, the Bible. When you read a book, it's much more meaningful if you personally know the author. Jesus is the Author and Finisher of your faith! Would you like to know Him?

If you've never accepted Jesus as your Saviour and would like to, please refer to pages 142 and 143 for a powerful prayer to lead you into a personal relationship with Him.

Introduction

THE POWER OF YOUR WORDS

Are words important? Do they really make a difference? Are there benefits to speaking specific words over yourself? The answer is yes!

A lady suffered from an ongoing fever. Doctors put her through a series of tests but found nothing physically wrong. What they did find is that, whenever she got angry, she would say, "That just burns me up!" They suggested she stop saying that. She stopped and the fever disappeared.

"I was scared to death."

"This dessert is to die for!"

"It's a pain in the neck."

Have words like that ever come out of your mouth? What if you actually get what you say?

Your words matter. They are like seeds that will produce a harvest, for good or bad.

"...if you choose to add a signal - for example, saying something like, 'My mother had depression and that's why I have depression, and now my daughter is suffering from depression,' then the epigenetic marks are activated. The thinking and speaking out the problem serve as the signal that makes it a reality." Dr. Caroline Leaf, Cognitive Neuroscientist, and Author of *Switch On Your Brain: The Key to Peak Happiness, Thinking and Health.*

This book is a compilation of words that you *should* be saying. Say what God says about you. If you're still unsure if your words matter, take a look at what the Bible reveals about the power of words.

"In the beginning God created the heaven and the earth. And God *said,* "Let there be light:" and there was light." (Genesis 1:1,3 KJV) Note God created the world with His *words.* God said...and it was so.

"In the beginning was the *Word,* and the *Word* was with God, and the *Word* was God. All things were made by him; and without him was not any thing made that was made. And the *Word* was made flesh, and dwelt among us..." (John 1:1,3,14a)

Jesus is the *Word,* personified. He created the world by speaking; so words can create. You are made in God's image and have been given the privilege and responsibility of speaking. Use your words for good. A word of encouragement could change someone's life.

The book of Proverbs gives practical truths and points out criteria regarding our speech. Note the following examples:

"Death and life are in the power of the tongue..." (Proverbs 18:21a)

"He that keepeth his mouth keepeth his life: but he that openeth wide his lips shall have destruction." (Proverbs 13:3)

There can be a voice of pride. "The king spake, and said, 'Is not this great Babylon, that I have built for the house of the kingdom by the might of my power, and for the honour of my majesty?' While the word was still in the king's mouth, there fell a voice from heaven, saying, 'O king Nebuchadnezzar, to thee it is spoken; The Kingdom is departed from thee.'" (Daniel 4:30,31)

The repercussions of speaking proud words caused this king to lose his mind and the ability to speak. He began to act like an animal.

"There is that speaketh like the piercings of a sword: but the tongue of the wise is health." (Proverbs 12:18)

"Sound speech, that cannot be condemned." (Titus 2:8)

The Lord hates a lying tongue and a false witness that speaks lies. (See Proverbs 6:16-19.)

Some may think they can say anything at all, without consequence. But in Psalm 12, David points out the speech of ungodly people: "They speak vanity every one with his neighbour: with flattering lips and a double heart do they speak. The Lord shall cut off all flattering lips, and the tongue that speaketh proud things: Who have said, "With our *tongue* will we prevail; *our lips are our own*: who is lord over us?" (Psalm 12:2-4)

"Thou art snared [caught, trapped] with the words of thy mouth..." (Proverbs 6:2)

"A soft answer turneth away wrath, but grievous words stir up anger. The tongue of the wise useth knowledge aright, but the mouth of fools poureth out foolishness. A wholesome tongue is a tree of life..." (Proverbs 15:1,2,4a)

"Put away from thee a froward [contrary] mouth, and perverse lips put far from thee." (Proverbs 4:24)

The old saying, "Sticks and stones may break my bones but words will never hurt me" is a lie. The truth is that words can deeply wound. "The words of a talebearer are as wounds, and they go down into the innermost parts of the belly." (Proverbs 18:8)

Good words, on the other hand, are healing.

"Pleasant words are as a honeycomb, sweet to the soul, and health to the bones." (Proverbs 16:24)

"A word fitly spoken is like apples of gold in pictures of silver." (Proverbs 25:11)

"She [the virtuous woman] openeth her mouth with wisdom; and in her tongue is the law of kindness." (Proverbs 31:26)

"A man hath joy by the answer of his mouth: and a word spoken in due season, how good is it!" (Proverbs 15:23)

The psalmist said, "Let the redeemed of the Lord say so, whom he hath redeemed from the hand of the enemy." (Psalm 107:2)

"Let my mouth be filled with thy praise and with thy honour all the day." (Psalm 71:8)

Jesus showed how powerful words of faith are. "And Jesus answering saith unto them, 'Have faith in God. For verily I *say* unto you, that whosoever shall *say* unto this mountain, Be thou removed, and be thou cast into the sea; and shall not doubt in his heart, but shall *believe* that those things which he *saith* shall come to pass; he shall have whatsoever he *saith*. Therefore I *say* unto you, what things soever ye desire, when ye pray, *believe* that ye receive them, and ye shall have them.'" (Mark 11:22-24)

"We having the same spirit of faith, according as it is written, I believed, and therefore have I spoken; we also believe, and therefore speak." (2 Corinthians 4:13)

Jesus said, "...for out of the abundance of the heart the mouth speaketh... But I say unto you, that every idle word that men shall speak, they shall give account thereof in the day of judgment. For by thy words thou shalt be justified and by thy words thou shalt be condemned." (Matthew 12:34-37)

We will give account for every idle word! Yikes! Where's the duct tape? If we have been speaking badly, we can repent, and ask for God's forgiveness and help to change what we say.

Speaking your faith is how you become a Christian. "That if thou shalt confess with thy mouth the Lord Jesus, and shalt believe in thine heart that God hath raised him from the dead, thou shalt be saved. For with the heart man believeth unto righteousness; and with the mouth confession is made unto salvation." (Romans 10:9,10)

Every time the devil tempted Jesus, Who never sinned, Jesus quoted a verse of Scripture, saying, "It is written..." The devil had to leave. God's Word is also *your* weapon against the devil's tactics. "For the Word of God is quick [living], and powerful, and sharper than any two-edged sword..." (Hebrews 4:12a)

The book of James, Chapter 3, shows that putting a tiny bit in a horse's mouth can turn its whole body. A huge ship can change direction with a very small helm. The tongue, though small, can cause great damage.

"Even so the tongue is a little member, and boasteth great things. Behold, how great a matter a little fire kindleth! And the tongue is a fire, a world of iniquity; so is the tongue among our members, that it defileth the whole body, and setteth on fire the course of nature; and it is set on fire of hell. Therewith bless we God, even the Father; and therewith curse we men, which are made in the similitude of God. Out of the same mouth proceedeth blessing and cursing. My brethren, these things ought not so to be. Speak not evil one of another, brethren." (James 3:5,6,9,10, James 4:11a)

"For he that will love life, and see good days, let him refrain his tongue from evil, and his lips that they speak no guile..." (1 Peter 3:10)

"Let your speech be always with grace, seasoned with salt, that ye may know how ye ought to answer every man." (Colossians 4:6)

"I create the fruit of the lips..." (Isaiah 57:19a)

Pray this prayer from Psalm 141:3. "Set a watch, O Lord, before my mouth; keep the door of my lips."

These Scriptures show that your words are important and produce fruit.

So what should you be saying? Say what God says! Put God's words in your mouth. Speak His Word aloud over yourself and over every situation. Be aware of what you say. Some words are simply habit. Ask God to check you if you're about to say something you shouldn't.

1

I Am Known by God

Isn't it your heart's cry, to be completely known and understood? God knows you and understands you. He knew you before you were born, because He planned you.

You are not an accident, a mistake or unwanted. God created you intentionally.

He knows everything about you, your thoughts, your dreams, your fears. He knows how many hairs are on your head!

"But the very hairs of your head are all numbered." (Matthew 10:30)

Grab a Bible and read Psalm 139 aloud. It is God's love letter to you. Meditate on God's intimacy. He really knows you!

"O lord, thou hast searched me and known me." (Psalm 139:1)

God thinks about you so much. His thoughts of you are more in number than the sand on the seashore! He knows when you sit down and when you stand up. He watches over you when you sleep and when you awake. He is always with you. Darkness cannot hide you from Him. He saw you being formed in the womb, and recorded all your fingers and toes! You are fearfully and wonderfully made.

No one in the world knows you like God. You are special to Him.

Everyone wants someone with whom they can share their journey in life, even in the smallest details. God is there for you. He cares about all you are going through.

Say aloud, "God planned me and knew me before I was born! He knows everything about me. I am special to Him."

2

I Am Loved

Studies have shown that babies who were fed and changed but not cuddled, are termed, 'failure to thrive.' The children lose weight and do not grow. This is a common condition found in some orphanages or institutions where there are not enough caregivers to give the individual attention required. We were born with the need to be loved.

When people feel unloved, it affects their self-worth and how they relate to others.

That's why people look desperately for love, even in destructive ways. Today, "I love you," is often just a line used to get something. It has no substance, no truth. Some think they are "in love" but may just feel emotional infatuation. So what is love?

Real love gives. Real love sacrifices for someone else. Real love is committed.

The problem is, many attempt to get their love tank filled by other people, who are also trying to get their love tank filled. Imperfect humans fail. They sometimes let you down. Look for love from the One Who is love: God. His love never fails.

You will never know who you really are or how much you are loved and valued, until you know God's love for you.

"God, who is rich in mercy, for his *great love* wherewith he loved us..." (Ephesians 2:4)

You are greatly loved by the One Who made you.

"We love him, because he first loved us." (1 John 4:19)

"Herein is love, not that we loved God, but that he loved us, and sent his Son [Jesus] to be the propitiation [to make us right with God] for our sins." (1 John 4:10)

"For God *so loved* the world, that he *gave* his only begotten Son, that whosoever believeth in him, should not perish, but have everlasting life." (John 3:16)

For centuries man has wrestled with his own identity and tried to comprehend God. Then God sent Jesus to shout to the world, "I love you!"

Imagine the One Who created the mountains, the moon, and the universe *loves you*! That's Christianity 101: Love.

In Jeremiah 31:3, the Lord says, "...I have loved thee with an everlasting love."

Say, "God loves me!" Say it again, "God loves me!" Say it all day long. Say it daily, until you get it. See if it doesn't make you smile, maybe even laugh.

3

I Am Accepted

As a kid, were you the last one picked for the baseball team? Ever feel like that now? Someone else gets the promotion, while you are overlooked. You may be in a room full of people, yet feel alone, unnoticed. We all want to be accepted. That's why some lower their standards, just to be a part of 'The Group'.

*When you **believe** that **Jesus** came to save you, and **personally receive Him** as your Lord, you are accepted by God!*

Then, when God looks at you, He sees you clothed with the robe of Christ's righteousness.

"...wherein he hath made us accepted in the beloved." (Ephesians 1:6b)

"For the Kingdom of God is not meat and drink; but righteousness, and peace, and joy in the Holy Ghost. For he that in these things serveth Christ is acceptable to God, and approved of men." (Romans 14:17,18)

It means turning your whole life over to God. Yield your body to God as a living sacrifice, holy, acceptable unto God. See Romans 12:1.

Jesus said, "All that the Father giveth me shall come to me; and him that cometh to me I will in no wise cast out." (John 6:37)

You don't need to follow the crowd to be accepted. Follow God!

Ask Him to give you great friends. He has all the contacts! As a Christian, you are part of a world-wide group, which is growing all the time. You don't have to work and strive to be accepted.

Through Jesus, God has already accepted you. You belong!

Say, "I receive Jesus as my Lord and Saviour. Now I'm accepted by God!"

4

I Am God's Daughter/Son

At age nine, I attended Vacation Bible School and watched the movie, *Pilgrim's Progress*. A pilgrim named Christian was trying to find his way to the Heavenly City. On his back, he carried a cumbersome burden, representing his sin. Christian faced many challenges along the way until, finally, he came to the Cross, where Jesus hung, dying for the sins of the world. Christian said, "Lord, I believe."

His heavy load of sin rolled off his back and down the hill. When I saw that, I thought, *That's what I need.* I went home, knelt by my bed, and asked Jesus to forgive my sins, come into my life and be my Saviour and Lord. At that moment, I became His child—part of the family of God!

"But as many as received him, to them gave he power to become the sons of God, even to them that believe on his name." (John 1:12)

"For ye are all the children of God by faith in Christ Jesus."
(Galatians 3:26)

Maybe you didn't have a good father or didn't even know your father. Your heavenly Father is not like that. He's not an uncaring, absentee father. He loves you, cares about you, and will never leave you!

You may be an orphan or feel like an orphan. If you have the heart of an orphan, you will only know how to love those who love you. Even though people are loving to you, you may reject the love, yet, at the same time, crave love. When you realize you are God's child, and loved for who you are, then you can freely love others.

"When my father and my mother forsake me, then the Lord will take me up." (Psalm 27:10)

God is the father of the fatherless. Read Psalm 68:5.

If you have never received God's love or His gift of salvation through Jesus, you can do it right now. Then confess Jesus as your Lord:

Say, "I'm a child of God. God is my loving Father. He will never leave me."

5

I Can Be Forgiven

Some people let their sin stop them from coming to God. They think they have to clean up their act before they can come to Him. But that's why God sent Jesus!

Come to Him just as you are. You must repent (be sincerely sorry and willing to turn from your sin). Humbly ask God for forgiveness, believing that Jesus took your punishment for you on the cross. Then confess with your mouth that Jesus is your Lord.

The moment you ask God for it, forgiveness is instant. Your spirit is born again. However, your mind and flesh need to be reprogrammed. Surrender your whole life to God and let Him change you into the excellent person He knows you can be. Becoming that person is a process, and it is achieved by daily seeking Him, reading His Word, applying it, and being led by His Holy Spirit, not by your flesh. (See *I Have the Power to Live the Christian Life, #17*)

King David was used mightily by God. Yet he sinned greatly. He committed adultery with a married woman, then arranged her husband's murder. His sin cost him the life of his little son. But David repented. Read his prayer in Psalm 51. Here's a sample that you can pray for yourself:

"Wash me thoroughly from mine iniquity, and cleanse me from my sin. For I acknowledge my transgressions... Hide Thy face from my sins, and blot out all mine iniquities. Create in me a clean heart, O God; and renew a right spirit within me."

"If we confess our sins, he is faithful and just to forgive us our sins, and to cleanse us from all unrighteousness." (1 John 1:9)

"Repent ye therefore, and be converted, that your sins may be blotted out, when the times of refreshing shall come from the presence of the Lord." (Acts 3:19)

"For thou, Lord, art good, and ready to forgive; and plenteous in mercy unto all them that call upon thee." (Psalm 86:5)

Hebrews 1:3 says that Jesus, "by himself purged our sins," clearing us of guilt.

There is only one condition to be forgiven: you must forgive others.

Jesus said, "For if ye forgive men their trespasses, your heavenly Father will also forgive you. But if ye forgive not men their trespasses, neither will your Father forgive your trespasses." (Matthew 6:14,15)

You may think you can't forgive someone, but forgiveness is a decision, not a feeling. God can enable you to forgive others. (See the next devotional: *I Can Forgive Others*)

Say, "I repent of sin and I receive God's forgiveness. I choose to forgive everyone. Now I'm forgiven!"

6

I Can Forgive Others

Pulling small weeds from a garden is easy. If left unattended, they develop a strong root system which is much harder to remove. It's the same with unforgiveness. If you choose to forgive an offense right away, it's fairly easy. But the longer you hold a grudge, replay the offense over and over in your mind, think and speak evil of the person, the harder it becomes to forgive. Unforgiveness then becomes a root of bitterness, a stronghold—and bondage.

In any relationship, you will have the opportunity to get offended. Then you have a choice. You can forgive, and be free; or you can hold a grudge. **A major tool of the devil is unforgiveness.** Don't fall for his trap.

"To whom ye forgive any thing, I forgive also…for your sakes forgave I it in the person of Christ; Lest Satan should get an advantage of us: for we are not ignorant of his devices."
(2 Corinthians 2:10,11)

Beware of the devil's setups. He uses people to hurt people. He stirs up strife, anger, and division, but he can only do so if you allow it. So foil the devil. Forgive! Pray for your enemies. Love them. Let God, the Judge, deal with them. Don't fight people, fight the devil.

Tell God all about it, including your hurt feelings. Ask Him to heal your wounds. Then say, "God loves me. God is for me. God values me."

"But I can't forgive them for what they did!" you may say.

If you don't forgive, you are spiritually tied to that person and this allows the person to continue to hurt you. When you forgive, and release them to God, it sets **you** free!

But they don't deserve to be forgiven! Maybe not. Yet who does? When anyone sins, they don't *deserve* to be forgiven. Think of Jesus, Who, although completely innocent, allowed His own creation to torture and murder Him. He didn't deserve that! Yet what did He say as He suffered on the cross? "Father, forgive them; for they know not what they do." (Luke 23:34)

The gospel is grace—the undeserved favour and love of God. When He forgives you, it's grace—God extending mercy you don't deserve. Likewise, He calls you to show mercy to others.

Holding onto unforgiveness can block answers to prayer. It can block healing. Take the high road. Choose to forgive, by an act of your will. Don't wait until you *feel* like it. It has nothing to do with emotions. When the hurt surfaces say, "I choose to forgive _____ (say their name)," You can even write it down, including the date you forgave them.

When Jesus was verbally abused, He did not retaliate, but committed Himself to God. Do not repay evil for evil, but rather bless the one who has done you wrong. You will receive a blessing. Read 1 Peter Chapters 2 and 3.

"Great peace have they which love thy law: and nothing shall offend them." (Psalm 119:165) Even taking offense is sin. Choose to be unoffendable. Love instead.

"Be ye kind one to another, tenderhearted, forgiving one another, even as God for Christ's sake hath forgiven you." (Ephesians 4:32)

Say, "I choose to forgive all who have hurt me. I won't carry the burden any longer. I give them to God. I choose to love. Now I'm free."

7

I Am a New Creation

Did you ever mess up and wish you could just start over? You can! If you think you've sinned so much that God wouldn't want you, you need these liberating truths.

When you receive Christ as your Saviour and Lord, you become a new person. Just as you take off your dirty clothes, have a cleansing shower, and put on fresh, clean clothes, when you surrender to Jesus, you put off the old sinful way and put on godly character. Christ makes you new. The old you died with Christ; now you live as a brand new creation as you allow Christ to live through you.

"But put ye on the Lord Jesus Christ, and make not provision for the flesh, to fulfill the lusts thereof." (Romans 13:14)

"Therefore if any man be in Christ, he is a new creature: old things are passed away, behold, all things are become new." (2 Corinthians 5:17)

"I am crucified with Christ, nevertheless I live; yet not I, but Christ liveth in me: and the life which I now live in the flesh I live by the faith of the Son of God, who loved me, and gave himself for me." (Galatians 2:20)

Isn't that amazing? To think that the Creator of the universe loves you so much that He gave His life for you!

"For ye are dead, and your life is hid with Christ in God. When Christ, who is our life, shall appear, then shall ye also appear with him in glory." (Colossians 3:3,4)

"And they that are Christ's have crucified the flesh with the affections and lusts." (Galatians 5:24)

"...the truth is in Jesus: That ye *put off* concerning the former conversation the old man, which is corrupt according to the deceitful lusts; And *be renewed in the spirit of your mind*; And that ye *put on* the new man, which after God is created in righteousness and true holiness." (Ephesians 4:21b-24)

Before you come to know Jesus, you do whatever your flesh "feels" like doing. This can produce trouble, heartache, and often hurts other people. But when you give your life to Christ, He becomes Lord. His Holy Spirit convicts you of sin. Now, when you feel tempted, you get a *check* in your spirit. You need to obey the Holy Spirit, ask for His help to resist temptation and do what is right. You have His power living inside you!

Your job is to submit to Him. Yield to Him. Let Him be boss. It's just like a soldier in the army, when given a command, says: "Yes sir!" You are a brand new person in Christ. You can start over. As you renew your mind with these truths and speak them out, your flesh will be retrained and you will experience the blessing of obedience. See yourself as brand new.

Say, "My old sinful self is dead. Now Christ lives through me and makes me new."

8

I Am Righteous in God's Eyes

Some people think that if they do enough good works, they will get into heaven. But think about that for a moment. How many good works would it take to erase all your sins, and make you as holy as God? Humanly speaking, it can't be done. The Bible says that, compared to God's measure of holiness, all our good works are like filthy rags. That's why He sent His Son, the perfect, sinless One, to pay for our sins.

The moment you receive Christ as your substitute, He takes your sins and gives you His righteousness. What a great trade! Jesus' work was completed at the cross. He said, "It is finished." He totally paid for your sins by taking the Father's wrath and judgment (which your sins deserve) upon Himself. Your part is to acknowledge Jesus as your Saviour. Now when the Father looks at you, He sees you as righteous—as if you had never sinned. You need to see yourself as righteous, not because of any good works you have done, but because Jesus' blood cleanses you from all sin, and makes you righteous.

I remember one time I closed my eyes and saw a picture of myself standing before God's throne. In His holy presence, I felt unworthy. I looked down, ashamed. Then I remembered that, because of Jesus, I'm covered with the robe of righteousness!

"I will greatly rejoice in the Lord, my soul shall be joyful in my God; for he hath clothed me with the garments of salvation, he hath covered me with the robe of righteousness...." (Isaiah 61:10)

"For he hath made him [Jesus] to be sin for us, who knew no sin; that we might be made the righteousness of God in him." (2 Corinthians 5:21)

"Being filled with the fruits of righteousness, which are by Jesus Christ, unto the glory and praise of God." (Philippians 1:11)

"And be found in him, not having mine own righteousness, which is of the law, but that which is through the faith of Christ, the righteousness which is of God by faith:" (Philippians 3:9)

"Not by works of righteousness which we have done, but according to his mercy He saved us, by the washing of regeneration, and renewing of the Holy Ghost." (Titus 3:5)

Jesus gave you His righteousness. Now live righteous by yielding to Him.

"If ye know that he is righteous, ye know that every one that doeth righteousness is born of him." (1 John 2:29)

Say, "I believe Jesus took my sins. I'm now righteous in God's eyes!"

9

I Am Made in God's Image
and He Fulfills Me

Worried about your self-image? Don't be! You were created by the Master Designer, in His own image (likeness). That makes you important! It means you are valuable and you represent God.

"So God created man in his own image, in the image of God created he him; male and female created he them. And the Lord God caused a deep sleep to fall upon Adam, and he slept: and he took one of his ribs, and closed up the flesh instead thereof; And the rib, which the Lord God had taken from man, made he a woman, and brought her unto the man. And Adam said, "This is now bone of my bones, and flesh of my flesh: she shall be called Woman, because she was taken out of Man." (Genesis 1:27, 2:21-23)

Are you constantly striving for fulfillment? Maybe you try to find satisfaction in a relationship, job, car, house, or hobby. Perhaps you continually try something new, hoping another location or the next exciting event will make you happy. But when you get what you thought would fulfil, there's still a longing for more. Something is missing. Where can you find fulfillment then?

If your life is a puzzle, Jesus is the missing piece.

Until you find Him, you won't be complete. In your life is a void that only He can fill. Be fulfilled by the One Who made you, knows you, loves you and has great plans for you.

Make Jesus your everything and you will discover He is all you need.

When you desire Jesus more than anything, you will be satisfied. And, when you delight in Him, He will give you your heart's desires.

"Delight thyself also in the Lord: and he shall give thee the desires of thine heart." (Psalm 37:4)

"He will fulfill the desire of them that fear Him: He also will hear their cry, and will save them." (Psalm 145:19)

"Seek ye first the Kingdom of God, and his righteousness; and all these things shall be added unto you." (Matthew 6:33)

"For in him [Christ] dwelleth all the fullness of the Godhead bodily. And ye are complete in him, which is the head of all principality and power." (Colossians 2:9,10)

Spend time with Jesus, get to know Him; then you will discover who you really are. You were made in His image, so reflect Him. Use your words, abilities and life to honour Him. Let His joy, peace and love shine from your face.

Say, "I'm made in the image of God, so I matter. Only He fulfills me."

10

God Lives in Me

Culture says your worth depends on your looks, the name brand of your jeans, or the style of your shoes. But that's a lie. Do you only have worth when you look fabulous? If you have a bad hair day, does your value decrease? Come on! You are valuable because of who you are, not your outward appearance. To God, you are of great worth.

When an angel told Mary that she would be the mother of Jesus, the Messiah, she must have been amazed. For nine months she actually had God Himself living inside her!

The moment you receive Jesus as your Saviour and Lord, God comes to live inside you, by His Holy Spirit. Your body becomes His temple! Get a revelation of that. What a privilege and responsibility. So it's important what you do with your body. Since God made you, and Jesus bought you with His own precious blood, you belong to Him. Your body must represent Him. That means dressing modestly. You can be fashionable and modest too. Sometimes you will have to go against the latest trend. So start a new trend! Be fun, fashionable, and covered! You are not an object for sale, to be lusted after or to be used, but rather a treasure, to remain pure for your husband or wife in marriage.

The Bible gives warning to run away from fornication (sexual sin). Every other sin is outside the body; but if you sin sexually, you actually sin against your own body.

"What? Know ye not that your body is the temple of the Holy Ghost which is in you, which ye have of God, and ye are not your own? For ye are bought with a price: therefore glorify God in your body, and in your spirit, which are God's."
(1 Corinthians 6:19,20)

In Bible days, only the priests could enter into the Holy of Holies in the Temple. When Jesus died on the cross, the veil in the temple ripped in two, giving everyone personal access to God. You don't need any person to go between you and God; only Jesus. Now you can pray to the Father in Jesus' name.

When you receive Jesus as your Lord, His Holy Spirit lives in you. That means you can do greater things than Jesus did!

Jesus said, "Verily, verily, I say unto you, He that believeth on me, the works that I do shall he do also; and greater works than these shall he do; because I go unto my Father." (John 14:12)

Think of that. You can do more miracles than Jesus did when He was on earth! Since He returned to heaven, He sent His own Spirit to come and make His home in you. You now have His power living in you.

The One Who lives inside you is more powerful than the devil. You don't have to allow the devil any access to your life.

"...greater is he that is in you, than he that is in the world."
(1 John 4:4b)

Be *God-inside* minded. Let Him live His life through you.

Say, "God lives in me. I am not my own. I am His temple."

11

If I Have Strayed, I Can Return to God

Have you left the church? Turned away from God? Become hardened against religion and those who believe? Perhaps you have run—like Jonah—in the opposite direction, away from God's calling. Maybe you have joined the world in its thinking and lifestyle. In your heart, you know what is right.

You may feel you are too far gone for God to take you back now.

That's what the devil wants you to think. But that's a lie.

Remember the prodigal son in Luke 15? He demanded his inheritance early, deserted his father, and ran away from home to do his own thing. He lived it up with his friends until all his money was gone. When his money ran out, so did his "friends". The good life came to an abrupt end. He got a job feeding swine. He was so hungry that he considered eating what the pigs were eating. This young man had hit rock bottom.

The Bible said he came to himself. In other words, he realized what he was really like, and how he had sinned. The wandering son was filled with regret. He remembered that back home even the servants were feasting on delicious food. So he humbled himself and returned home, planning to work as one of his dad's hired hands, thinking he no longer qualified to be a son.

Mustering up his courage, he walked up the lane to his old homestead. Suddenly, he saw his father look up and recognize him. The son almost turned back. But then he saw his father running toward him, arms opened wide.

"Son! Welcome home!" His dad embraced and kissed him, despite his dirty hair, filthy clothes, and terrible smell. His father told him how he had been watching and waiting for him every day. Then his father called for the best robe, a ring for his son's finger, shoes for his feet, and threw him a dinner party! The dad declared that his son was dead, but now is alive again. He was lost, but now is found.

The father's unconditional love and mercy triumphed over justice. Regardless of what the young man had done, he would always be his father's son!

Like this earthly father, God is watching and waiting for you to come back to His loving arms.

"Return, ye backsliding children, and I will heal your backslidings. Behold, we come unto thee, for thou art the Lord our God." (Jeremiah 3:22)

If you have run from God, it's time to come home. God is willing to forgive and forget.

Tell God you're sorry. Ask for His forgiveness. Return to God. He loves you.

Say, "I will stop running away from God, and return to His loving arms."

12

I Can Overcome Rejection

The original scam artist, the devil, is guilty of identity theft, even among Christians. He whispers negative, demeaning, lying thoughts into your mind, trying to undermine your true identity. Sometimes those lies seem so real that you may mentally and verbally agree. When you do that, it gives the lies power over you.

The enemy uses people as well—often those closest to you, like family members or those in authority over you—to hurt, shame, or simply devalue your worth. These hurts can crush self-esteem and open the door to the spirit of rejection. This can lead to a lifetime of approval addiction, deception, fear, jealousy, unforgiveness, and other habitual sins.

Past hurts can trigger harmful reactions, like emotional outbursts, withdrawal, putting up walls, and ending relationships to protect oneself from further hurt.

If you don't know your true identity from God, then you may attempt to get it from people, whose opinions fluctuate like the blowing wind. If one is insecure, then a look or a word from a relative, friend, even a stranger can cause you to feel rejected, and the cycle repeats. Even perceived rejection is damaging, as you imagine the negative things that another person may be thinking of you.

Feelings of inferiority, insecurity, failure, or not measuring up can cause many problems with inter-personal relationships, whether in marriage, on the job, or in social settings. The person suffering with the delusion of rejection will be constantly striving to gain acceptance and approval from others to feel better about himself or herself. It's a futile race, like a hamster running madly in a wheel…going nowhere.

Ask God to show you how much He loves, accepts, and esteems you. When you really get that revelation, it will be life-changing and freeing.

No more striving. No more fear of people. You find your identity, security, and worth in the One Who made you. If the One Who made the universe says you're okay, who can argue? Then you can face the world with a whole new outlook, with confidence, and with love. When you know you are loved, you can extend love to others. You can smile. You are special to God!

"If God be for us, who can be against us?" (Romans 8:31b)

"The Lord is on my side; I will not fear: what can man do unto me? The Lord taketh my part with them that help me… It is better to trust in the Lord than to put confidence in man." (Psalm 118:6-8)

Say, "God loves me. God accepts me. God is for me!"

13

I Am Clean

God looks beyond our sin to our potential in Him. When we sincerely repent and turn from sin to Him, He will wash away all that sin by the precious blood of His Son, Jesus.

In 1 Corinthians 6:9,10, God gives a long list of sinners who will not be allowed into heaven. Yet, if they repent, turn from their sins, and live for Jesus, then God makes them clean.

"And such were some of you: but ye are washed, but ye are sanctified, but ye are justified in the name of the Lord Jesus, and by the Spirit of our God." (1 Corinthians 6:11)

"But if we walk in the light, as he is in the light, we have fellowship one with another, and the blood of Jesus Christ his Son cleanseth us from all sin." (1 John 1:7)

"As far as the east is from the west, so far hath he removed our transgressions from us." (Psalm 103:12)

"Come now, and let us reason together, saith the Lord: though your sins be as scarlet, they shall be as white as snow; though they be red like crimson, they shall be as wool." (Isaiah 1:18)

When a person becomes saved, God washes the sins away. But the devil will try to bring sins back to your mind and into your life again. Resist him.

"Submit yourselves therefore to God. Resist the devil, and he will flee from you." (James 4:7)

One way to resist the devil is to quote aloud God's Word over the situation.

If you sin, confess and forsake it right away, so it does not get a foothold in your life. You want to maintain a right relationship with the Lord.

"If we confess our sins, he is faithful and just to forgive us our sins and to cleanse us from all unrighteousness." (1 John 1:9)

Say, "I turn away from my sin and confess it to Jesus. Now I'm clean!"

14

I Am Safe

Do rules limit or protect? Rules can literally save your life. When God put Adam and Eve in the Garden of Eden, they literally *had it all*. Everything was beautiful and plentiful. There was only one rule. Don't eat of that one tree over there; it will kill you. If only they had listened to God—not their own reasoning, not the lies of the devil—how different this world would be! God gives us instructions for our own good.

"And the Lord commanded us to do all these statutes, to fear the Lord our God, for our good always, that he might preserve us alive..." (Deuteronomy 6:24)

Preserve means to keep alive, safe from harm or injury.

"Hear my voice, O God, in my prayer: preserve my life from fear of the enemy." (Psalm 64:1)

In these dangerous times, it's wise to ask the Lord where to go, when, and which route to take. You want to be at the right place at the right time, not in harm's way. Speak this verse before you head out: (Personalize the quote by saying me or my.) "The Lord shall preserve thee from all evil: he shall preserve thy soul. The Lord shall preserve thy going out and thy coming in, from this time forth, and even for evermore." (Psalm 121:7,8)

"The Lord preserveth all them that love him..." (Psalm 145:20a)

"And the Lord shall deliver me from every evil work, and will preserve me unto his Heavenly Kingdom: to whom be glory for ever and ever. Amen." (2 Timothy 4:18)

Regarding safety, watch your words. Don't say negative things. "I'm so tired, I'll probably have a car accident." "It gave me a heart attack!" "That drives me crazy." "What else can go wrong?" A seemingly innocent phrase can open the door for the enemy.

"...the lips of the wise shall preserve them." (Proverbs 14:3b)

Read Psalm 91 and Psalm 121. Daily claim those promises and the protective blood of Jesus over yourself and your family, home, vehicles, and pets.

"No weapon that is formed against thee shall prosper..." (Isaiah 54:17a)

"...safety is of the Lord." (Proverbs 21:31b)

"For he shall give his angels charge over thee, to keep thee in all thy ways." (Psalm 91:11)

"The name of the Lord is a strong tower: the righteous runneth into it, and is safe." (Proverbs 18:10) If you only have time to call out, "Jesus!" He will be on the scene.

"I will never leave thee, nor forsake thee." (Hebrews 13:5b)

"...I am with you always, even unto the end of the world. Amen." (Matthew 28:20b)

"I will fear no evil: for thou art with me." (Psalm 23:4b)

Say, "God is always with me, keeping me safe."

15

I Love God Most

What takes most of your time and attention? Your boyfriend/girlfriend? Technology? Making money? Problems? Kids? Anything can become an idol. Is your focus on someone or something other than God?

God wants first place in your life.

"Jesus said unto him, Thou shalt love the Lord thy God with all thy heart, and with all thy soul, and with all thy mind." (Matthew 22:37) This is the greatest command.

Notice the word *all*. God wants all of you. He wants your complete devotion. Jesus said if you love Him, you will obey Him.

God is not an add-on to your life. He *is* your life! God supplies your next breath! Without Him you can do nothing. See John 15:5. He is not to be kept in your pocket until your next crisis. Your life is to be about Him, about His agenda. When you put God first, and love others, He will bless you abundantly.

"And he is the head of the body, the church: who is the beginning, the firstborn from the dead; that in all things he might have the preeminence." (Colossians 1:18)

Eminence means a high rank. Preeminence means to put before others. Put God before people, career, pleasure, even before yourself. If you have put someone or something before God, confess it to Him. Tell God you want to put Him first.

With so many distractions to take your attention off God, it's easy to forget Him. So how do you put Him first? Schedule a daily appointment with Him, maybe first thing in the morning. Plan your day around Him, instead of trying to squeeze Him into your agenda. God longs to fellowship with you. It's an amazing privilege!

Unplug. Turn off the phone, computer and TV. Get quiet. Focus on God. It will give you true perspective in life.

"Be still, and know that I am God." (Psalm 46:10a)

Get to know God. Enjoy Him. Sing to Him. Tell Him you love Him. Thank Him. Inquire where to read in the Bible and allow Him to speak to you. As you establish this daily habit, you will begin to crave His Presence like He wants yours. Be conscious of Him all day. Talk to Him about everything and listen for Him.

God created you for intimacy. In the Garden of Eden, Adam and Eve enjoyed complete, close fellowship with the Lord. They chatted together as they strolled along in God's beautiful creation, watching the deer graze and the swans glide across the water. It was perfect fellowship with one another and with their Creator, just as God intended.

"Acquaint now thyself with him, and be at peace: thereby good shall come unto thee." (Job 22:21)

"Thou wilt shew me the path of life: in thy presence is fullness of joy; at thy right hand there are pleasures for evermore." (Psalm 16:11)

"Draw nigh [near] to God, and he will draw nigh to you." (James 4:8a)

Say, "I will spend time in God's presence daily and love Him most of all."

16

I Am Loving

Love is essential for interpersonal relationships. First you must realize how much God loves you with His perfect love. (See *I am Loved*, #2) When you are secure in God's love, then you can love others.

God loved us even when we rebelled against Him. Love doesn't wait for the other person to reciprocate or change. Real love is a choice, a decision that is not based on feelings, or on how another person acts. True love is loyal. Love sacrifices for another. Love forgives.

"Beloved, let us love one another: for love is of God; and every one that loveth is born of God, and knoweth God. He that loveth not knoweth not God; for God is love." (1 John 4:7,8)

God is love. If we don't love others, we don't truly know God.

So what is real love?

"Charity [love] suffereth long [is very patient with difficult people], and is kind; charity envieth not, charity vaunteth not itself [is not vain], is not puffed up [in pride], doth not behave itself unseemly, seeketh not her own, is not easily provoked, thinketh no evil." (1 Corinthians 13:4,5)

Personalize this by speaking over yourself: "I am patient and kind; I'm not envious…"

To understand how to receive and give love, study and apply these Scriptures:

1st John Chapters 1-4   1 Corinthians 13:4-7
Romans 13:8-10   Luke 10:25-37
St. John 14:23,24   St. John 15:1-17

It's easy to love those who love you, but Jesus said to love your enemies. Do good to them that hate you. How do we love like that? Through the power of the Holy Spirit! You can't control others, but you can control yourself, by yielding to the Holy Spirit. (See *I Have the Power to Live the Christian Life*, #17)

Love is a fruit of the Spirit. With God's ability, you *can* love the unloving. Ask Him to give you His love for them. If someone is hard to love, ask God, "Lord, how would You respond to this person?" He will answer!

"Beloved, if God so loved us, we ought also to love one another. And we have known and believed the love that God hath to us. *God is love*; and he that dwelleth in love dwelleth in God, and God in him. There is no fear in love; but *perfect love casteth out fear*: because fear hath torment. He that feareth is not made perfect in love." (1 John 4:11,16,18)

God commands us to love Him most, and love others as we love ourselves. Doing that keeps all Ten Commandments. Jesus said love fulfills God's law.

Love never fails! *1 Corinthians 13:8a*

Say, "Love Himself, lives in me. I yield to His love for others."

49

17

I Have the Power to Live the
Christian Life

Do you want to do what is right, but often fail? Do you feel frustrated? There is a spiritual battle between your flesh (the old you) and your born again spirit. Your flesh desires to do whatever it wants, with no thought of consequence. Your spirit wants to do what is right to please God, but the question is *how?* Read Romans Chapter 6.

The answer is through Holy Spirit power! You can't live the Christian life without God's help. Ask the Lord to fill you with His Spirit and bear His fruit in you.

"Be not drunk with wine, wherein is excess; but be filled with the Spirit." (Ephesians 5:18)

The Holy Spirit is a gentleman, Who will not force you to do His will. He needs to be invited, reverenced and obeyed. He can be hurt. Yet when you allow Him to lead, you will have overcoming power in your life!

"If we live in the Spirit, let us also walk in the Spirit." *(Galatians 5:25)*

Read all of Galatians Chapter 5. To walk in the Spirit means to keep in step with Him. Be sensitive to His leading. He is the still, small voice that will direct you, convict you, and comfort you.

"Walk in the Spirit, and ye shall not fulfil the lust of the flesh. But the fruit of the Spirit is love, joy, peace, long-suffering, gentleness, goodness, faith, meekness, temperance [self-restraint]." (Galatians 5:16, 22,23)

Simply yield to the Holy Spirit Who lives in you! He is the One with the power to enable you to live righteously. Do not quench or grieve the Holy Spirit; instead, submit to Him.

"Quench not the Spirit." (1 Thessalonians 5:19)

"And grieve not the holy Spirit of God, whereby ye are sealed unto the day of redemption." (Ephesians 4:30)

"For if ye live after the flesh, ye shall die: but if ye *through the Spirit* do mortify [put to death] the deeds of the body, ye shall live." (Romans 8:13)

After Jesus died on the cross and came back to life, He told His followers that He was going back to heaven, but He would send the Comforter to them. He told them to wait, and they would receive power after the Holy Ghost (Spirit) came upon them. Then they could witness for Him. Just as the disciples needed Holy Spirit power, so do you. His power enables you to live the Christian life. Yield to Him moment by moment, and allow Him to work.

Say, "I am Holy Spirit-powered!"

18

I Work For the Lord

Do you ever feel unappreciated? Do you have a difficult boss? Remember who you really serve. The Lord sees all you do. Don't do your work only for money, a person or a company. Choose to do everything for the Lord. He is your true boss. Be diligent and enthusiastic. Work with all your might. You will feel great for a job well done.

"And whatsoever ye do in word or deed, do all in the name of the Lord Jesus, giving thanks to God and the Father by Him. Servants, obey in all things your masters according to the flesh; not with eye-service, as menpleasers; but in singleness of heart, fearing God; and whatsoever ye do, do it heartily, as to the Lord, and not unto men; knowing that of the Lord ye shall receive the reward of the inheritance: for ye serve the Lord Christ." (Colossians 3:17,22-24)

You serve the LORD! He will reward you.

"Not slothful [lazy] in business; fervent in spirit; serving the Lord." (Romans 12:11)

Do you procrastinate and put off jobs that seem too big? Maybe you don't even know where to start. Ask the Lord for help. Set the timer for 15 minutes. If you need to organize your office, start with one drawer. When you get victory over that, it will motivate you to do more. You can do it! Getting started is the hardest part. Once you dive in, you'll be glad you did. Lethargy reaps lethargy, and diligence reaps diligence.

"Only fear the Lord, and serve him in truth with all your heart: for consider how great things he hath done for you." (1 Samuel 12:24)

"...choose you this day whom ye will serve...but as for me and my house, we will serve the Lord." (Joshua 24:15)

You are called to serve. Look at those around you. If you see a need, fill it. Even Jesus came not to be served, but to serve. John 13 records that Jesus, our Lord and Master, took a basin of water and a towel, then washed the disciples' feet. What a lowly task for the King of kings! Yet the Lord said He did it as an example for us to follow.

Say, "In whatever I do, I do my best for the Lord."

19

I'm a God-pleaser, Not a People-pleaser

Do you worry what others think of you? Are you a people-pleaser? Perhaps you feel good about yourself only when people approve of you. Constantly striving to get your worth from others can be exhausting. People are fickle. One day they may like you, but the next they'll ignore you. The question is,

Do you have value only when people like you?

Now that's a funny thought. Of course not! Yet for a people-pleaser, this can seem like truth.

Whether you are in high school, college, the business world, or work at home, there is probably a person or group from whom you seek approval. To get that desired approval, you may act like a chameleon—changing your colour, so to speak—by the way you dress, how you talk, and what you do, in order to fit in. The problem is, you are not being true to yourself and, if you are a Christian, you are not being true to God.

"For do I now persuade men, or God? Or do I seek to please men? For if I yet pleased men, I should not be the servant of Christ." (Galatians 1:10)

Jesus asked, "How can you believe, which receive honour one of another, and seek not the honour that cometh from God only?" (John 5:44)

You may have been abused or put down by family or peers. Maybe you feel like you don't measure up, or that you're not smart enough, good enough, pretty enough. Those are lies. God created you in His image! He is **for** you. Since your fingerprints and DNA are different than those of anyone else in the world, it means you are special. Unique. Why try to be a carbon copy of someone else?

You can break approval addiction. Even if you've been like this for years, you can change. It's time to be set free. Get the truth. Change your thinking.

In order to find your real worth, you need to look to God alone. Make time to seek Him and search His Word. Faith pleases God. He rewards those who diligently seek Him. Read Hebrews 11:6. Ask God to show you who you really are in Christ.

What value does God put on you? You are worth the precious blood of Jesus! God considers you worth dying for!

Once you realize your true value, you won't feel the need to impress others to gain self-esteem. You can relax and be yourself. It's truly freeing! Others will be drawn to the "real" you. As you take off your mask, they will feel free to be genuine and share their struggles.

The bottom line is, who are you living for? People? Yourself? Or God? Make a choice. Live to please the Lord. Have a new mindset. Get your mind off yourself, and focus on God. Don't be **self**-conscious, be **God**-conscious.

Say, "I live to please God, not people."

20

I Am Created For God

When God created mankind, it was for family. He longs to love you, bless you, and share your life in daily fellowship. In return, you are to live for Him.

God has a great plan and purpose for your life—much greater than you could imagine. When frustrations, disappointments, or problems come, remember Jesus is your reason for living. That puts things into proper perspective, and returns your focus to God, Who is well able to handle any problem.

"For of him, and through him, and to him, are all things: to whom be glory for ever. Amen." (Romans 11:36)

"...all things were created by him, and for him." (Colossians 1:16b)

In his book, "This is Our Love," Pastor Jody Cross features a song by worship leader Dan Macaulay. It's called, *From You, For You.* Dan believes we are to use what we've been given and love those around us with those gifts.

On a baseball team, each person has a specific position and must work together to win. Like the human body, each part has a role to play. Just because the eyes may look beautiful doesn't mean they are more important than the feet.

So in Christ's body, known as the Church, each believer has a job to do. Christ is the Head and He gives each one of us gifts and abilities to be used for Him, and to benefit others.

"For we are his workmanship, created in Christ Jesus unto good works, which God hath before ordained that we should walk in them." (Ephesians 2:10)

"Now ye are the body of Christ, and members in particular." (1 Corinthians 12:27)

What gifts has God given you? Are you musical? Do you enjoy baking? Are you a hands-on server? A teacher? If unsure, ask God what your gifts are and how to use them to serve others.

Say, "I will use my talents for God."

21

I Am More Than a Conqueror

Through Jesus, we have victory in this world. He has defeated the enemy and given us power over him.

If a school bully was after your son, think how quickly the bully would back off if the teacher stepped up beside your child. You need to picture God on your side, against every bully out there. You can live confidently, knowing that God is for you.

"Nay, in all these things, we are more than conquerors through him that loved us." (Romans 8:37)

The Bible says Satan is the accuser. He wants to bring back all our past failures and sins. But if we have trusted Jesus' finished work on the cross, the devil has nothing on us. Jesus even made a public display of him, ridiculing him. The devil thought he had gotten rid of Jesus, but Jesus triumphantly rose from the dead, foiling the wicked one's plan.

"Blotting out the handwriting of ordinances that was against us, which was contrary to us, and [Jesus] took it out of the way, nailing it to his cross; and having spoiled principalities and powers, he made a show of them openly, triumphing over them in it." (Colossians 2:14,15)

"Now thanks be unto God, which always causeth us to triumph in Christ..." (2 Corinthians 2:14a)

"Through God we shall do valiantly: for he it is that shall tread down our enemies." (Psalm 108:13)

"When I cry unto thee, then shall mine enemies turn back: this I know; for God is for me." (Psalm 56:9)

"If God be for us, who can be against us?" (Romans 8:31b)

"The Lord is on my side; I will not fear: what can man do unto me? The Lord taketh my part with them that help me..." (Psalm 118:6,7a)

Jesus said, "Behold, I give unto you power to tread on serpents and scorpions, and over all the power of the enemy: and nothing shall by any means hurt you." (Luke 10:19)

You have power over all the power of the devil through Jesus. You have victory through what Jesus did at the Cross. You can use Jesus' name, His Blood, His Word, and the power of the Holy Spirit to resist this foe. The enemy is defeated. That makes you a winner.

Say, "I live in victory with God on my side."

22

I Am Not Conformed to This World

"And be not conformed to this world: but be ye transformed by the renewing of your mind, that ye may prove what is that good, and acceptable, and perfect will of God." (Romans 12:2)

The world is reaping the effects of a civilization that has turned its back on God. Being a Christian today isn't easy. Standing up for what is right and living by the Bible is the opposite of the world's mindset. There is a spiritual battle going on and it's coming to a climax.

The only way to be salt and light in this world is to stay in tune with the Lord, and to be in His Presence and in His Word daily. Meditating on God's Word will renew your mind in the truth. Then you can steer clear of counterfeits. Ask the Holy Spirit to fill you, give you discernment and go with you into every situation. Pray for His peace at meetings, in traffic, and at home.

Do not let yourself copy what the world is doing. Choose not to talk like the world or act like the world. That means you won't watch the movies or listen to the music with the majority. Choose godly movies and music. Be set apart, consecrated to the Lord. Don't do anything you wouldn't do if Jesus was sitting beside you.

"Love not the world, neither the things that are in the world. If any man love the world, the love of the Father is not in him. For all that is in the world, the lust of the flesh, and the lust of

the eyes, and the pride of life, is not of the Father, but is of the world. And the world passeth away, and the lust thereof: but he that doeth the will of God abideth for ever." (1 John 2:15-17)

"Set your affection on things above, not on things on the earth." (Colossians 3:2)

"Pure religion and undefiled before God and the Father is this, to visit the fatherless and widows in their affliction, and to keep himself unspotted from the world." (James 1:27)

"...our Lord Jesus Christ Who gave himself for our sins, that he might deliver us from this present evil world, according to the will of God and our Father." (Galatians 1:3b,4)

"But God forbid that I should glory, save in the cross of our Lord Jesus Christ, by whom the world is crucified unto me, and I unto the world." (Galatians 6:14)

What would have happened if Noah had followed the crowd and conformed to the sinful world? Think how difficult it was for him to withstand the name-calling, social pressure, and opposition during the building of the mammoth ark. His focus was on God, not the world. Thankfully he stayed strong. Only Noah and his family lived...while the rest of the world died in the flood.

Jesus asked, "For what shall it profit a man, if he shall gain the whole world, and lose his own soul? Whosoever therefore shall be ashamed of me and of my words in this adulterous and sinful generation; of him also shall the Son of man be ashamed, when he cometh in the glory of his Father with the holy angels." (Mark 8:36,38)

Say, "I will not conform to this world. I will follow God's ways."

23

I Am Reaching My Goal

The God Who made you has a plan for your life. He has given you the abilities, talents, and everything you need to fulfill your purpose. You have a specific call on your life. Ask God what it is. He is not trying to hide it from you. Spend time in prayer and seek His will; then be available to Him. Let Him show you His plan. He may not show you the end result, but when you take a step, He will guide you to the next step. When He tells you to do something, do it. Trust and obey. Let Him work in and through you.

"Being confident of this very thing, that he which hath begun a good work in you will perform it until the day of Jesus Christ." (Philippians 1:6)

"For I know the thoughts that I think toward you, saith the Lord, thoughts of peace, and not of evil, to give you an expected end." (Jeremiah 29:11)

"For it is God which worketh in you both to will and to do of his good pleasure." (Philippians 2:13)

"And we know that all things work together for good to them that love God, to them who are the called according to his purpose." (Romans 8:28)

"I also labour, striving according to his working, which worketh in me mightily." (Colossians 1:29)

Seek God every day. Ask for His agenda. As you purpose to follow Him and do His will, you will find great satisfaction and joy. He will open doors for you that no man can shut.

Each day can be an adventure as you listen for the Holy Spirit to direct your path and show you what to accomplish that day. God sees everything you do and will reward you. Keep pressing on.

"I press toward the mark for the prize of the high calling of God in Christ Jesus." (Philippians 3:14)

Say, "Step by step, I am achieving God's will for my life."

24

I Am Free

Freedom. We all want to be free. Yet many fall prey to the enemy's deception and traps. The liar says, "Do whatever you feel like! Be free!" But while he offers something that looks or feels good in the moment, there is deadly poison in the bait. Instead of freedom, it's bondage. Slavery. Then the addictive chains of sin wrap around the victim so tightly that there appears to be no hope of breaking free. The devil is a cruel taskmaster. He lied to Adam and Eve, broke their intimacy with God, stole their real identity, their dominion over the earth, their life in paradise, and caused them to experience pain and the journey towards death. The enemy is still using the same bag of tricks on people today.

But there is a way to be free.

Finding God's truth, meditating on it, speaking it, and obeying it is the path to freedom. That is the reason for this book. By finding the truths that counter Satan's lies, speaking it over yourself and putting God's Word into practice, you can break free of any addiction or stronghold. You can know who you really are in Christ, and the authority you have over the enemy.

Jesus said, "If ye continue in my Word, then are ye my disciples indeed; and ye shall know the truth, and the truth shall make you free. If the Son therefore shall make you free, ye shall be free indeed." (John 8:31,32,36)

"For he that is dead is free from sin." (Romans 6:7) Your old sinful self died when you made Jesus your Lord and Saviour.

"For the law of the Spirit of life in Christ Jesus hath made me free from the law of sin and death." (Romans 8:2)

"Stand fast therefore in the liberty wherewith Christ hath made us free, and be not entangled again with the yoke of bondage." (Galatians 5:1)

"And I will walk at liberty: for I seek thy precepts." (Psalm 119:45)

It's time to replace
lies with truth,
fantasy with reality,
lust with love,
darkness with light.

Shine the spotlight of God's truth on the dark deception of the devil and he will flee!

Say, "I'm no longer in bondage, because Jesus' truth sets me free!"

25

I Rejoice With Singing

Rejoicing, singing, and praising God is to be a lifestyle, not only to worship Him, but for your own benefit too. There are 150 psalms [songs] in the Bible.

"I will sing unto the Lord as long as I live: I will sing praise to my God while I have my being. My meditation of him shall be sweet: I will be glad in the Lord." (Psalm 104:33,34)

"This is the day which the Lord hath made, we will rejoice and be glad in it." (Psalm 118:24) "Rejoice in the Lord always: and again I say, rejoice." (Philippians 4:4)

It's easy to rejoice when things are going well. But it's also important to rejoice when life is hard. Read Habakkuk 3:17-19. Here the farmer had crop failure and lost his livestock, which meant no income. But he wasn't moved by his circumstances. He said, "Yet I will rejoice in the Lord, I will joy in the God of my salvation." (verse 18)

Rejoicing in the Lord can turn things around. It will lift your mood, even before you see things change. If you let a situation get you down, it can cause you to be immobilized and do nothing. Instead, make the choice to rejoice! Rejoicing is a powerful weapon against the enemy, who wants to steal your joy and your strength.

"...for the joy of the Lord is your strength." (Nehemiah 8:10b)

Being upset, worried or gloomy will not help the situation or you. So rejoice in the Lord, the Faithful One. He has the power to change things. When experiencing problems, give it all to God, thank Him, then return to peace and joy. This is so important.

Troubled King Saul sent for David, who played his harp for him. Then the evil spirit left.

"Thou art my hiding place; thou shalt preserve me from trouble; thou shalt compass me about with songs of deliverance." (Psalm 32:7) Music and singing can change the atmosphere and other people; it can also deliver you. Try humming a tune when you're with others. They may start humming too.

We need joy for health and strength. How are we to rejoice? Smile, laugh, sing, dance, clap, jump up and down. Even if you don't *feel* like rejoicing, feelings follow the actions. Start counting your blessings. Be thankful. Soon you'll think, "What problem?"

"I will sing a new song unto thee, O God..." (Psalm 144:9a) It's fun to create your own song and sing to God from your heart; create a brand new, original love song to Him. Put a smile on God's face. He also wants to see joy on your face.

God is rejoicing and singing over you. "The Lord thy God in the midst of thee is mighty; he will save, he will rejoice over thee with joy; he will rest in his love, he will joy over thee with singing." (Zephaniah 3:17)

"Serve the Lord with gladness: come before his presence with singing." (Psalm 100:2)

Even if you can't sing, you can "Make a joyful *noise* unto the Lord..." (Psalm 100:1) He will love it.

Why not sing through your day today?

Say, "I will rejoice in the Lord always! I will sing to Him."

26

I Can Memorize God's Word

"Thy word have I hid in mine heart, that I might not sin against thee." (Psalm 119:11)

Hiding God's Word in your heart means memorizing Bible verses. Do this, and the Holy Spirit can bring it to your mind when you need it. God instructs us to meditate (ponder, contemplate, to consider carefully and thoroughly) on the Word day and night, in order to do what it says, which brings blessings.

"This book of the law shall not depart out of thy mouth; but thou shalt meditate therein day and night, that thou mayest observe to do according to all that is written therein: for then thou shalt make thy way prosperous, and then thou shalt have good success." (Joshua 1:8) Read the Word. Think it. Memorize it. Speak it. Do it.

While working full-time, I'd escape the office by driving into the countryside to eat my lunch and read a book on how to share Jesus with others. It included Bible verses to memorize. I loved hiding God's Word in my heart. I even won a prize (homemade fudge!) for memorizing the most verses at Bible class. I still remember those verses today.

"But his delight is in the law of the Lord; and in his law doth he meditate day and night. And he shall be like a tree planted by the rivers of water, that bringeth forth his fruit in his season; his leaf also shall not wither; and whatsoever he doeth shall prosper." (Psalm 1:2,3)

If your Bible was suddenly confiscated, how much would you remember?

The best way to memorize Scripture is to pick one verse and write it on a card. Read the verse slowly, grasping the full meaning. Now focus on one phrase. Repeat the phrase over and over until you've got it. Do the same with the next phrase until you have covered the whole verse. Then say the verse all together. Include the reference, so you can always locate the verse in your Bible. Keep the card with you and review it during the day. Soon it will be hidden in your heart—where no one can steal it!

Memorizing Scripture will become a treasure. You will love the Word of God!

Say, "Every day, I hide God's Word in my heart."

27

When I Talk to God, He Hears Me

"Pray without ceasing." (1 Thessalonians 5:17)

Pray nonstop? How do you do that? Keep a running conversation with God during the day. Invite Him into each decision, each activity. Enjoy His fellowship. Get to know Him and enjoy Him. You can learn to be aware of God and include Him in your life. Yet it's important to have a specific time of prayer as well.

Find a place to pray. It may be your closet, a favourite chair, or a private room for your daily, intimate time with the Lord. You can tell God anything. Tell Him what is troubling you and what gives you joy. Then listen to Him. Get quiet and let Him speak to you.

"But thou, when thou prayest, enter into thy closet, and when thou hast shut thy door, pray to thy Father which is in secret; and thy Father which seeth in secret shall reward you openly." (Matthew 6:6)

Choose a time. You may be a morning person or perhaps you like evenings best. As you make room in your agenda for important things, schedule a daily appointment with the Lord. Give it priority.

"Trust in him at all times; ye people, pour out your heart before him: God is a refuge for us." (Psalm 62:8)

"And he [Jesus] spake a parable unto them to this end, that men ought always to pray, and not to faint." (Luke 18:1) Pray for your family, community and country. You can also pray with others. "Confess your faults one to another, and pray one for another, that ye may be healed. The effectual fervent prayer of a righteous man availeth much." (James 5:16)

"If my people, which are called by my name, shall humble themselves, and pray, and seek my face, and turn from their wicked ways; then will I hear from heaven, and will forgive their sin, and will heal their land." (2 Chronicles 7:14)

"And this is the confidence that we have in Him, that, if we ask any thing according to His will, He heareth us: and if we know that he hears us, whatsoever we ask, we know that we *have* the petitions that we desired of Him." (1 John 5:14,15)

Jesus said, "And all things, whatsoever ye shall ask in prayer, *believing,* ye shall *receive*." (Matthew 21:22)

"And whatsoever ye shall ask *in my name*, that will I do, that the Father may be glorified in the Son. If ye shall ask any thing *in my name*, I will do it." (John 14:13,14)

Our prayers are precious to God and He stores them up.

"And when He had taken the book, the four beasts and four and twenty elders fell down before the Lamb, having every one of them harps, and golden vials full of odours [fragrances], which are the prayers of saints." (Revelation 5:8)

You can also pray the Lord's Prayer. See Matthew 6:9-13.

"Call unto me, and I will answer thee, and show thee great and mighty things, which thou knowest not." (Jeremiah 33:3)

Say, "When I pray, God hears and answers my prayers."

28

I Am Thankful

"In every thing give thanks: for this is the will of God in Christ Jesus concerning you." (1 Thessalonians 5:18)

Give thanks in everything? Seriously? That's what the Bible says. It sounds illogical. Yet it worked for me.

I had been praying and grieving over a situation for six long months. Although nothing had changed, finally I said, "Thank You, Lord, that this happened."

A short time later, things totally turned around for good. This time my thanks was heartfelt! The Lord told me that my thanksgiving is what changed things. When you have trials, give thanks.

Obedience to God's Word pays rewards, even when it doesn't seem to make sense. God's principles work and, when followed, will produce the desired results.

"O give thanks unto the Lord, for he is good: for his mercy endureth for ever." (Psalm 107:1)

"It is a good thing to give thanks unto the Lord, and to sing praises unto thy name, O Most High." (Psalm 92:1)

"O give thanks unto the Lord; call upon his name: make known his deeds among the people." (Psalm 105:1)

Give thanks for family members as well. It's easy to take them for granted. We hear amazing eulogies at a funeral; yet they are too late for the person to hear. Why not tell them now? Give them flowers now. Tell them you are thankful for them and why. Praise their attributes. Write it in a card. Send a text. It only takes a few moments, yet it could be transforming for both of you.

"I thank my God upon every remembrance of you, always in every prayer of mine for you all making request with joy." (Philippians 1:3,4)

Give God thanks for your health, abilities, job, friends, home, all of His blessings. Thank Him for speaking to you through the Bible and the ability to talk to Him in prayer.

"Enter into his gates with thanksgiving, and into his courts with praise: be thankful unto him, and bless his name." (Psalm 100:4)

Be thankful in every season; let thanksgiving be year round!

Say, "I give thanks to God in everything."

29

God is My Healer

If you are sick, ask God what to do, spiritually and physically. If you need medical help, ask God to give the doctor wisdom. Get believers to pray. Speak God's Scriptures on healing out loud over yourself daily.

God says, "*Attend to my Words*; incline thine ear unto my sayings. Let them not depart from thine eyes; keep them in the midst of thine heart. For they are *life* unto those that find them, and *health* to all their flesh." (Proverbs 4:20-22)

"*Bless the Lord, O my soul, and forget not all his benefits: Who forgiveth all thine iniquities, who healeth all thy diseases; Who redeemeth thy life from destruction...*" (Psalm 103:2-4a) Personalize this by saying "my" life, etc.

"Himself [Jesus] took our infirmities, and bare our sicknesses." (Matthew 8:17b)

"He [God] sent his word and healed them, and delivered them from their destructions." (Psalm 107:20)

"A merry heart doeth good like a medicine: but a broken spirit drieth the bones." (Proverbs 17:22) Be joyful!

"I shall not die, but live, and declare the works of the Lord." (Psalm 118:17)

There is no sickness too difficult for God to heal. Jesus went about preaching the gospel and healing *all* manner of sickness and *all* manner of disease. See Matthew 4:23.

When Jesus was asked to heal, He always said, "*I will.*"

"And Jesus said unto him, I will come and heal him." (Matthew 8:7)

It is still His will to heal today, for He does not change.

"Jesus Christ, the same yesterday, and today and forever." (Hebrews 13:8)

When King Hezekiah was dying, he sought the Lord for healing. God sent the prophet Isaiah to tell him, "Thus saith the Lord, the God of David thy father, I have heard thy prayer, I have seen thy tears: behold, I will heal thee." (2 Kings 20:5) Then Isaiah told him to take a lump of figs and put it on the boil and he recovered.

Sickness can be caused by sin, unforgiveness, worry, fear, poor diet, stress, toxins, negative thinking, inadequate sleep, lack of exercise, even wrong words. Seek the Lord on what to change. Repent of all sin. Forgive everyone. Take proper care of your body. Don't be uptight. Say, "There will be no dis-ease in me. I have God's peace and joy."

Speak to your body. You can say, "Immune system, be built up and fight off every germ, virus, and sickness." Jesus spoke to the fig tree and it heard and obeyed him! How much more will your body respond to the sound of your own voice. Tell the pain or sickness to leave, and healing to come. If you speak negatively, your body will respond to that too. Don't say, "I'm catching a cold," or "It's flu season and I always get the flu." Never say, "Diabetes runs in my family." No! Stop it with your words! Say what the Word of God says instead.

It's as easy for God to heal sickness as to forgive sins. Healing gives God glory.

Jesus asked, "Whether is it easier to say to the sick of the palsy, Thy sins be forgiven thee; or to say, Arise, and take up thy bed, and walk?" Then Jesus healed the lame man. And immediately he arose, took up the bed, and walked, so they were all amazed, and *glorified God*. Read Mark 2:9,12.

"Beloved, I wish above all things, that thou mayest prosper and be in health, even as thy soul prospereth." (3 John 2)

Say, "Thank You, Jesus, for providing my healing. I receive it by faith."

30

I Will Not Fear

Fear is not from God.

"For God hath not given us the spirit of fear; but of power, and of love, and of a sound mind." (2 Timothy 1:7)

Fear comes from the devil. Those negative 'what if' thoughts are darts from the enemy. Just as you resist the devil, you can resist fear. Refuse to fear! Put up your shield of faith and quench those darts. Do not speak or think about the fear-based circumstance.

Fear is a lie. Here's an acronym. F-E-A-R: **F**alse **E**vidence **A**ppearing **R**eal.

Get the truth of God's Word to combat the lies. Speak the promises of God aloud.

"Fear not!" This command from the Lord is repeated over and over in the Bible. And if He tells you not to fear, then it is possible.

"Fear thou not; for I am with thee: be not dismayed; for I am thy God: I will strengthen thee; yea, I will help thee; yea, I will uphold thee with the right hand of my righteousness." (Isaiah 41:10)

"...that through death he [Jesus] might destroy him that had the power of death, that is, the devil; and deliver them who through fear of death were all their lifetime subject to bondage." (Hebrews 2:14b,15)

Fear is bondage. Jesus is the Deliverer.

"I sought the Lord and he heard me and delivered me from all my fears." (Psalm 34:4)

With Jesus asleep in the boat, His disciples panicked when a violent storm arose. They woke Him, asking, "Don't You care that we're going to die?"

"And he [Jesus] arose, and rebuked the wind, and *said* unto the sea, 'Peace, be still.' And the wind ceased, and there was a great calm. And he said unto them, 'Why are ye so fearful? How is it that ye have no faith?'" (Mark 4:37-40)

Faith in God and His Word is the anecdote to fear. Trust God.

"He shall not be afraid of evil tidings: his heart is fixed, trusting in the Lord." (Psalm 112:7)

Do you fear people? If you feel self-conscious or uncomfortable with people, *stop thinking of yourself* and think of them. Smile! Ask questions about their interests and family. People like to talk about themselves. Practice being a good listener. Seek to bless people.

Rest in the Lord. When fear tries to come, say, "God is for me. God loves me. God is with me." Remember who you are in Christ. You do not need to be a slave to fear anymore. God is bigger than any problem.

You may have had a problem with fear for years, so you avoid people or certain situations. This can be overcome! You can be free—free to be yourself—free to breathe. Know and meditate on how much God loves and esteems you. Perfect love casts out fear. See 1 John 4:7-21.

Say, "I will not fear. I put my trust in God!"

31

I Am Not Anxious

We live in a stress-filled world. Dealing with time pressure, work issues, people, rush hour traffic, responsibilities, family, and finances can seem overwhelming. Many people suffer physical ailments caused by stress. Our bodies were not designed to carry the burden of worry. A naturopath said, "It's better not to eat, than to eat when you are stressed."

If you feel tense, take a few deep breaths. Smile! Sing or hum a happy tune. Go outdoors for a walk. Look at some peaceful artwork or think of something funny or positive, like kittens playing.

"The Lord is my shepherd, I shall not want." (Psalm 23:1)

Charles L. Allen wrote a book called, God's Psychiatry. As a minister, he counselled many who came looking for relief from the stress and anxiety they were experiencing. Just as a doctor writes out a prescription, Rev. Allen prescribed the 23rd Psalm. The Psalm was to be read aloud (not just quoted from memory) upon awaking, directly after breakfast, lunch, dinner, and right before bed. It was to be read slowly, meditating on each verse. This was to be done for 7 days. The results were remarkable. Those who followed these instructions were no longer worried, nervous, or upset. They had peace, knowing that God was taking care of them, like a shepherd cares for his sheep. I have meditated on Psalm 23 myself, and it works.

Be aware of what you are thinking. You are always thinking about something, whether problems, concerns, people or positive thoughts. Really focus your thoughts on what is good, like the Word of God. Speak positive words like, "All is well. I have God's peace."

The power of the Word can calm any troubled soul—especially when it's spoken aloud. There is supernatural power when God's Word comes out of your mouth. Talk to God about everything. Hand over every problem.

"Be careful [full of cares, anxious] for nothing; but in every thing by prayer and supplication with thanksgiving let your requests be made known unto God. And the peace of God, which passeth all understanding, shall keep your hearts and minds through Christ Jesus." (Philippians 4:6,7)

Say, "I refuse anxiety. I give all my concerns to God and I yield to His peace."

32

I Grow Up in Christ

Babies cry for milk, not steak. When you first become a believer in Jesus, you start out as a spiritual baby. You need the basics of God's Word.

"As newborn babes, desire the sincere milk of the word, that ye may grow thereby." (1 Peter 2:2)

The Scriptures are able to make you wise and instruct you. As you feast on the Bible, it will cause you to grow, and soon you can digest the meat of the Word.

"All scripture is given by inspiration of God, and is profitable for doctrine, for reproof, for correction, for instruction in righteousness: that the man of God may be perfect, thoroughly furnished unto all good works." (2 Timothy 3:16-17)

"But speaking the truth in love, may grow up into him in all things, which is the head, even Christ." (Ephesians 4:15)

As you spend time with the Lord in prayer, read His Word, and fellowship with other believers, you will mature. You don't want to remain a baby Christian. You need to grow up in Christ. Let His Word and the conviction of the Holy Spirit change your character. Then you can fulfill God's call on your life and mentor others in the Lord.

"When I was a child, I spake as a child, I understood as a child, I thought as a child: but when I became a man, I put away childish things." (1 Corinthians 13:11)

A child is self-centered and must grow up and think of others. For many people in today's culture, life revolves around selfish desires. Love considers others and is not selfish. When a person has a problem or feels down, a great anecdote is to reach out and help someone else. It's amazing how gratifying, how fulfilling it is to give to others. So meet a need. Make someone's day.

Growing up is a matter of looking first to God and His Word, then looking around to see others' needs. That's love.

Say, "I will spend time with God and implement His Word, so I can grow up."

33

I Get Wisdom from God

Do you have decisions to make? Do you need wisdom? Ask God.

"If any of you lack wisdom, let him ask of God, that giveth to all men liberally, and upbraideth [criticizes] not; and it shall be given him. But let him ask in faith, nothing wavering." (James 1:5,6a)

The book of Proverbs has much to say about wisdom.

"The fear of the Lord is the beginning of wisdom: and the knowledge of the holy is understanding." (Proverbs 9:10)

Search for God's wisdom from His Word.

"My son, if thou wilt receive my words, and hide my commandments with thee; so that thou incline thine ear unto wisdom, and apply thine heart to understanding; yea, if thou criest after knowledge, and liftest up thy voice for understanding; if you seekest her as silver and searchest for her as for hid treasures; then shalt thou understand the fear of the Lord and find the knowledge of God. For the Lord giveth wisdom: out of his mouth cometh knowledge and understanding." (Proverbs 2:1-6)

It's not enough to accumulate a multitude of facts. A person needs God's wisdom to know how to apply them. Wisdom is better than silver and gold. All the things you can desire are not to be compared with it! There are many benefits from obtaining wisdom and understanding. God's wisdom brings long life, riches, honour, pleasantness, peace, and happiness. Read Proverbs 3.

"Happy is the man that findeth wisdom, and the man that getteth understanding." (Proverbs 3:13)

The principles in Proverbs are shown by contrasts. For example, a proud person brings shame, but the humble is wise.

"Wisdom is the principal thing; therefore get wisdom: and with all thy getting get understanding. Exalt her, and she shall promote thee: she shall bring thee to honour, when thou dost embrace her." (Proverbs 4:7,8)

Since there are 31 chapters in Proverbs, you can establish a habit of reading one chapter each day of the month. Apply these practical precepts to your life and watch the results.

Say, "When I ask God for wisdom, He will provide it."

34

I Stay Positive

"For all the promises of God in him are yea [yes], and in him Amen [so be it], unto the glory of God by us."
(2 Corinthians 1:20)

A positive outlook promotes inspiration, creativity, goal-setting and health.

Kick out negativity! It seems the human mindset gravitates naturally to the negative. Just listen to conversations. Constant complaints about the weather, the traffic, the slow service. You name it. It's easy to get into the bad habit of complaining. The next time you hear someone complain, try turning it around to the positive.

"What a rotten day. Nothing but rain!"

"Well, let's be thankful. It's better than freezing rain!"

God hates complaining. He takes it personally. Complaining shows ingratitude.

When the Israelite people complained, it displeased the Lord and made Him angry. They were destroyed because of their complaining! See Numbers 11:1.

"Do all things without murmurings and disputings."
(Philippians 2:14)

"...that there be no complaining in our streets." (Psalm 144:14b)

My mom, Eva, a registered nurse, didn't have an easy life, yet she purposely chose to see the good in the world and in people. She kept her sense of humour and looked on the bright side of life. She enjoyed simple pleasures, like going for a walk in the forest to gather wildflowers for the table. She knew how to make an ordinary day shine. Mom always thought of others. Her normal lifestyle was giving gifts and cards, as well as encouraging, helping, and blessing people. She never allowed negativity to affect her. She rose above it by staying positive and doing what was right.

Dave, my husband, blesses me daily with his upbeat attitude. "Life is what you make it," he says. He works hard, laughs a lot, enjoys life and delights to serve others. It's certainly more fun to be around someone who is happy than someone negative.

If you tend to see the glass half empty, try to look for the positive. Keep your mind on your amazing God. Retrain your brain to be optimistic.

Say, "I choose to think positive thoughts."

35

I Put Past Failures Behind Me

"...forgetting those things which are behind, and reaching forth unto those things which are before, I press toward the mark for the prize of the high calling of God in Christ Jesus." (Philippians 3:13,14)

In the book of Genesis we read that Joseph suffered much for many years of his life. His love and zeal for God made his jealous brothers despise him. They ripped the special coat his father gave him, threw him into a pit, plotted to kill him, but sold him to be a slave. In a foreign land, Joseph was falsely accused and put into prison, seemingly forgotten, until God redeemed him and made him overseer of the whole land. Joseph named his firstborn son Manasseh, which means *forgetting*, because God helped him forget the pain of the past.

Many people are stuck in neutral, paralyzed because of past hurts or failure. Their past ruins the present and blocks the future. Living in the past is like trying to drive a car forward while looking in the rear view mirror. That's a recipe for disaster.

Lay out your past before God. Give it all to Him. Repent of all sin. Receive God's forgiveness. Forgive those who have hurt you. Don't let your past hold you captive any longer. Move ahead. Ask God to heal you. Ask the Lord if you need to apologize to anyone; if so, how and when. Let Him lead you.

Once you confess and forsake your sin, God will forget it.

"...for I will forgive their iniquity, and I will remember their sin no more." (Jeremiah 31:34b)

"I, even I, am he that blotteth out thy transgressions for mine own sake, and will not remember thy sins." (Isaiah 43:25)

Don't let the devil condemn you. If you have received God's forgiveness, don't allow the enemy to keep bringing those sins to mind. Don't believe the lie that you've messed up too much or that God cannot use you. No matter what your past was like, God can redeem it.

Look at the people God used in His work: Moses was a murderer, David was an adulterer, Rahab was a prostitute. Yet when sin was confessed and forsaken, they were able to start again. God can still use you too.

When the past is taken care of, get excited about your future. Seek God and press into His good plans for you.

Say, "I no longer let my past dictate my future. With God, I can start fresh today."

36

I Live by Faith

We hear a lot about faith. What exactly is faith? Here's the Bible definition:

*"Now **faith** is the **substance** of things hoped for, the **evidence** of things not seen." (Hebrews 11:1)*

So faith is the substance (like physical matter) of godly things you desire, and the evidence (proof) of what you don't yet see. Since God cannot lie, we know His words are true. Therefore, we can trust in His promises, knowing they will come to pass.

Jesus said, "According to your faith be it unto you." (Matthew 9:29b)

Faith is belief in God's Word. Believe God's promises with your heart, and confess them with your mouth. That's the same way you get saved. See Romans 10:9,10.

As you immerse your mind, words and actions in the Word of God, your faith will grow! Faith is putting your confidence in God and His Word over what you see, how you feel, what others do, or the circumstance. Give God's Word the final say. Believe it. Trust it. Speak it. Obey it.

Living by faith is the only way to please God.

"But without faith it is impossible to please him: for he that cometh to God must believe that he is, and that he is a rewarder of them that diligently seek him." (Hebrews 11:6)

How do you get faith?

"...Faith cometh by hearing, and hearing by the word of God." (Romans 10:17)

"Whatsoever is not of faith is sin." (Romans 14:23b)

Are you lacking in faith?

Jesus said, "If ye had faith as a grain of mustard seed, ye might say unto this Sycamine tree, Be thou plucked up by the root, and be thou planted in the sea; and it should obey you." (Luke 17:6)

Jesus also said..."If thou canst believe, all things are possible to him that believeth." (Mark 9:23)

Does that mean believe anything? No, it means believe what God has said in the Bible.

Faith works by love. (See Galatians 5:6b)

In order for your faith to work, you must walk in love with others.

Say, "I live by faith. I believe God's promises in His Word are true."

37

I Abide in Jesus

If you chop off an apple tree branch, the branch cannot bear apples since it's no longer connected to the life-sustaining source.

Jesus said, "Abide in me, and I in you. As the branch cannot bear fruit of itself, except it abide in the vine; no more can ye, except you abide in me. I am the vine, ye are the branches: he that abideth in me, and I in him, the same bringeth forth much fruit: for without me ye can do nothing." (John 15:4,5)

One definition of abide means to live or remain. The Lord wants you to stay in close fellowship with Him, connected, through every part of your day. Talk to Him while mowing the lawn, driving, or doing laundry. Include the all-wise One in problem-solving and sharing your joys. When you abide in Jesus, you can do great things. You have the power of God living in you!

There is protection when we abide in Him.

"He that dwelleth in the secret place of the Most High shall abide under the shadow of the Almighty." (Psalm 91:1)

Abiding in the Lord keeps you from sin.

"And now, little children, abide in him; that, when he shall appear, we may have confidence, and not be ashamed before him at his coming." (1 John 2:28)

Look at Jesus' promise:

"If ye abide in me, and my words abide in you, ye shall ask what ye will, and it shall be done unto you." (John 15:7)

In your busyness, it's easy to compartmentalize life. One part for God, and the rest for your own tasks and pleasures. Have you ever put God *on hold* or maybe *ignore*? Jesus is your best Friend. He is eager to direct and bless you. He is just waiting for you to cling to Him so He can.

Say, "I abide in Jesus throughout my whole day!"

38

I Am Redeemed

The word *redeemed* means to buy back, to deliver, to bring out of bondage those who were kept prisoners by their enemies.

"Christ hath redeemed us from the curse of the law, being made a curse for us: for it is written, Cursed is every one that hangeth on a tree." (Galatians 3:13)

"And He saved them from the hand of him that hated them, and redeemed them from the hand of the enemy." (Psalm 106:10)

Some people think, "I'm my own boss." The truth is, we serve someone. Before a person comes to Christ, his master is the devil. He is in bondage to slavery, doing whatever the enemy of his soul wants him to do, by listening to the thoughts that the devil implants in his mind. Jesus came to rescue us from slavery!

Jesus said, "Whosoever committeth sin is the servant of sin. If the Son therefore shall make you free, ye shall be free indeed." (John 8:34,36)

He came to buy you back. Read what Jesus said to the Pharisees (the religious leaders of His day) in John 8:31-59. He told them that they followed their father, the devil, who is a liar.

"Looking for that blessed hope, and the glorious appearing of the great God and our Saviour Jesus Christ; Who gave himself for us, that he might redeem us from all iniquity, and purify unto himself a people..." (Titus 2:13,14)

Why would God, Who made the universe, come to suffer and die? He did it for you. Do you know how highly esteemed and valued you are? Jesus paid the price to redeem you, at great cost: with His own blood. That makes you very valuable. The Holy One took the punishment for sin that each person deserves. The just for the unjust. "In whom [Jesus Christ] we have redemption through his blood, the forgiveness of sins, according to the riches of his grace." (Ephesians 1:7)

"Their Redeemer is strong; the Lord of hosts is his name..." (Jeremiah 50:34a)

Jesus loves you so much! He is your Redeemer.

Say, "Jesus came to redeem me with His own precious Blood. I am highly valued!"

39

I Am Seated With Christ

"How are you today?" someone may ask. "I'm okay, under the circumstances." The truth is, if you are a Christian, you don't have to be *under* the circumstances. You have a new position in Christ.

Here's what the Bible says:

*"And what is the exceeding greatness of his power to usward who believe, according to the working of his mighty power, which he wrought in Christ, when he raised him from the dead, and set him at his own right hand in the heavenly places, **far above** all principality, and power, and might, and dominion, and every name that is named, not only in this world, but also in that which is to come: and hath put all things under his feet, and gave him to be the head over all things to the church."* (Ephesians 1:19-22)

*"But God, who is rich in mercy, for his great love wherewith he loved us, even when we were dead in sins hath quickened us [made us alive] together with Christ, (by grace ye are saved); and hath **raised us up** together, and **made us sit** together **in heavenly places in Christ Jesus**."* (Ephesians 2:4-6)

As you read the book of Ephesians, you will see many references to being *in Christ*. That changes your status.

When you became born again, your spirit was made brand new and you were given a new position. Since you are now *in*

Christ you are seated in the heavenlies with Him. That means you are above the problems.

You have Christ's perspective, as well as His authority and power available to you over earthly situations. This is the same power that raised Jesus from the dead! By speaking God's Word over the situation, pleading the blood of Jesus, and using the mighty name of Jesus, you can take authority over it!

You may want to read that again. Let it sink in. Doesn't that make you want to dance? God is so amazing, so AWESOME. Look what the Lord has done!

Say, "I'm raised up and seated in heavenly places in Christ and I have His power over every situation!"

40

I Wear God's Armour

A soldier going into battle must wear protective gear. He has to be on the lookout for the enemy. Since you have an invisible foe who comes to steal, kill, and destroy, you need to recognize his setups and tactics. Since he attacks the mind, and can work through words, you need to be aware of what you think and speak. Be armed and ready.

Look at Ephesians 6:11-17:

"Put on the whole armour of God, that ye may be able to stand against the wiles of the devil. For we wrestle not against flesh and blood, but against principalities, against powers, against the rulers of the darkness of this world, against spiritual wickedness in high places. Wherefore take unto you the whole armour of God, that ye may be able to withstand in the evil day, and having done all, to stand. Stand therefore, having your loins girt about with truth, and having on the breastplate of righteousness; and your feet shod with the preparation of the gospel of peace; above all, taking the shield of faith, wherewith ye shall be able to quench all the fiery darts of the wicked. And take the helmet of salvation, and the sword of the Spirit, which is the word of God."

The helmet of salvation means to be born again or saved, by accepting Jesus as your Lord and Saviour. The breastplate of righteousness covers the heart, the source of all the issues of life. The belt of truth overpowers the devil's lies. The shield of faith protects from the fiery darts of the wicked. The sword of the Spirit is the Word of God, a major weapon against the devil. That's why you must speak God's Word. The shoes of the gospel of peace are needed as you present Jesus to others who need to hear the gospel.

You fight a spiritual adversary. Don't give him any open door in your life. Never dabble in the occult. Don't watch or read evil material. Beware of the evil propaganda against children.

"Abstain from all appearance of evil." (1 Thessalonians 5:22)

Although the devil sometimes uses people against you, remember that people are not the enemy. Fight the devil, not people. Love, forgive and pray for people. The enemy is deceptive so you must always be on guard.

"Submit yourselves therefore to God. Resist the devil, and he will flee from you." (James 4:7)

Say, "Every day, I put on the armour of God. I resist the devil and he will flee."

41

Sin Does Not Have Dominion Over Me

Have you ever seen a dead person rob a bank? No! A dead person cannot sin. When you became a Christian, your old, sinful self died. Jesus raised you to new life in Him.

"Knowing this, that our old man is crucified with him, that the body of sin might be destroyed, that henceforth we should not serve sin. For he that is dead is freed from sin. Likewise reckon ye also yourselves to be dead indeed unto sin, but alive unto God through Jesus Christ our Lord. Let not sin therefore reign in your mortal body, that ye should obey it in the lusts thereof. Neither yield ye your members as instruments of unrighteousness unto sin: but yield yourselves unto God, as those that are alive from the dead, and your members as instruments of righteousness unto God. For sin shall not have dominion over you... Know ye not, that to whom ye yield yourselves servants to obey, his servants ye are to whom ye obey; whether of sin unto death, or of obedience unto righteousness? But now being made free from sin, and become servants to God, ye have your fruit unto holiness, and the end everlasting life." (Romans 6:6,7,11-14a,16,22)

Isn't that great news? Sin does not control you anymore. If you are Christ's, then the old sinful person was put to death. Now you need to yield your desires, body, and thoughts to God. If you yield to sin, you are the slave of sin. Christ has made you free—don't go back into bondage.

Who are you yielding to? The Lord or your flesh? Yield yourself to God.

You need to retrain your mind in the Word. Get rid of old mindsets and behaviours. That's the key. The next time you are tempted to repeat an old sinful habit, you can say, "No, I'm dead to that."

"...let us lay aside every weight, and the sin which doth so easily beset us, and let us run with patience the race that is set before us." (Hebrews 12:1b)

The enemy lies and says you'll never get victory over this sin, addiction, or ungodly relationship. But you can! Jesus defeated the devil. Now the enemy has no power over you, unless you give it to him. If you struggle with a repetitive sin or addiction, ask God for the power to say, "No!" Print out Bible verses that address the problem and post them around your house where you can see them, carry them with you, and speak them aloud. Each victory will lessen the enemy's hold.

Say, "Sin does not have dominion over me. I'm dead to sin! I'm alive to God!"

42

I Have Peace

Is life sometimes chaotic? Do you feel stressed? God doesn't want you to be uptight about anything. Give all of your problems to Him. Tell God everything. Ask for His help and His Word on the situation. Get a concordance or go online and find appropriate verses. Declare these promises aloud. Thank the Lord that He is working. Let Him handle it. Then return to peace and joy. Get your mind back on God, not problems.

"Thou wilt keep him in perfect peace, whose mind is stayed on thee: because he trusteth in thee." (Isaiah 26:3)

"Now the God of hope fill you with all joy and peace in believing, that ye may abound in hope, through the power of the Holy Ghost." (Romans 15:13)

"Now the Lord of peace himself give you peace always by all means. The Lord be with you all." (2 Thessalonians 3:16)

"Great peace have they which love thy law: and nothing shall offend them." (Psalm 119:165)

Jesus says do not allow your heart to be upset or fearful. Resist it.

Jesus said, "Peace I leave with you, my peace I give unto you: not as the world giveth, give I unto you. Let not your heart be troubled, neither let it be afraid." (John 14:27)

Jesus is the Prince of Peace. If you are born again, He lives in you by His Holy Spirit. Yield to the Holy Spirit. Let Him bear His fruit in you: love, joy, peace.

"Rest in the Lord..." (Psalm 37:7a)

Take some deep breaths. Smile. Laugh. Sip a cup of tea. Have a massage. Go for a walk. Play with a furry pet. Exercise. Have a bubble bath. Put on peaceful music. Hum. Read the psalms. Take some time for yourself. Relax!

Say, "I yield to the peace Jesus gives me."

43

I Am God's Witness

If you have received Jesus, then you are His walking billboard! Your life should be a godly example. Share Jesus with others. You are a beacon of light shining for Him, to help people come out of darkness.

You may say, but I'm afraid to talk to people about Jesus. I wouldn't know what to say. Ask the Holy Spirit to help you. All you have to do is open your mouth. He'll give you the words.

"But ye shall receive power, after that the Holy Ghost is come upon you: and ye shall be witnesses unto me both in Jerusalem, and in all Judea, and in Samaria, and unto the uttermost part of the earth." (Acts 1:8)

When you meet someone, smile at them. It will make them feel better. They might even smile back! But even if they don't, you have shown them kindness. Smiling reflects God's love and joy. It blesses others. Don't let the devil have your face space! Your expression should be a good witness. You represent the King of kings!

"And all things are of God, who hath reconciled us to himself by Jesus Christ, and hath given to us the ministry of reconciliation... God was in Christ, reconciling the world unto himself, not imputing their trespasses unto them; and hath committed unto us the word of reconciliation. Now then we are ambassadors for Christ, as though God did beseech you by us:

we pray you in Christ's stead, be ye reconciled to God."
(2 Corinthians 5:18-20)

"Ye are my witnesses, saith the Lord, that I am God."
(Isaiah 43:12b)

Water baptism is a type of witnessing. When you are
baptized, you are in obedience to the Lord. You publicly declare
your surrender to Christ. As you are submerged in water, then
come up out of the water, it symbolizes that your old, sinful self
is buried with Christ and you rise again to newness of life.

"Arise, shine; for thy light is come, and the glory of the Lord
is risen upon thee. For, behold, darkness shall cover the earth,
and gross darkness the people: but the Lord shall arise upon
thee, and his glory shall be seen upon thee." (Isaiah 60:1,2)

People are watching your life. Be ready to give the reason
you have hope, peace, and joy in the midst of troubled times.
It's Jesus!

Say, "I'm going to shine for Jesus and tell others about
Him."

44

I'm a Giver

Giving is a practical principle of God. It's the law of sowing and reaping. For God so loved, that He *gave* His only Son for us. What an investment! God sowed His Son Jesus to the world, and is still reaping the millions of souls that receive His free gift.

Jesus said, "Give, and it shall be given unto you; good measure, pressed down, and shaken together, and running over, shall men give into your bosom. For with the same measure that ye mete [measure out] withal it shall be measured to you again." (Luke 6:38)

God says to give to Him first, as a tithe (a tenth of your income), plus offerings, and then He will pour out blessings upon you. God isn't trying to take from you; He is trying to bless you. Spending God's money, the tithe, blocks blessings.

"Will a man rob God? Yet ye have robbed me. But ye say, Wherein have we robbed thee? In tithes and offerings. Ye are cursed with a curse: for ye have robbed me, even this whole nation. Bring ye all the tithes into the storehouse, that there may be meat in mine house, and prove me now herewith, saith the Lord of hosts, if I will not open you the windows of heaven, and pour you out a blessing, that there shall not be room enough to receive it. And I will rebuke the devourer for your sakes, and he shall not destroy the fruits of your ground; neither shall your vine cast her fruit before the time in the field, saith the Lord of hosts." (Malachi 3:8-11)

A man asked Jesus, "What shall I do to inherit eternal life?" Jesus told him to obey the commandments. The man said that he had. Jesus instructed him to go, sell everything he owned, give it to the poor, and follow Him. But the man was sad and went away grieved, for he had many possessions. This man loved his stuff more than he loved Jesus. (See Mark 10:17-22) This test revealed the condition of the man's heart. Do you love God more than money?

"For the *love of money* is the root of all evil: which while some coveted after, they have erred from the faith, and pierced themselves through with many sorrows. Charge them that are rich in this world, that they be not highminded, nor trust in uncertain riches, but in the living God, who giveth us richly all things to enjoy." (1 Timothy 6:10,17)

Money isn't evil. We all need money to live. It's the *love* of money that is the root of all evil. Don't let money and possessions be your god; that is dangerous. Put God first, and He will supply all of your needs. Use money to meet the needs of others.

"Blessed is he that considereth the poor: the Lord will deliver him in time of trouble. The Lord will preserve him, and keep him alive; and he shall be blessed upon the earth: and thou wilt not deliver him unto the will of his enemies." (Psalm 41:1,2)

"Every man according as he purposes in his heart, so let him give; not grudgingly, or of necessity: for God loveth a cheerful giver." (2 Corinthians 9:7)

"...Remember the words of the Lord Jesus, how he said, It is more blessed to give, than to receive." (Acts 20:35b)

Say, "I'm a cheerful giver!"

45

Jesus is My High Priest

The Bible says without the shedding of blood, there is no remission [forgiveness] for sin. I asked the Lord why. He reminded me that the wages of sin is death. That's how serious sin is. Sin earns death.

"For the wages of sin is death, but the gift of God is eternal life through Jesus Christ our Lord." (Romans 6:23)

In the Old Testament, God directed His people to offer blood sacrifices to atone for their sins. The sacrifice was usually a lamb. Only the High Priest could perform this task. He repeatedly made the sacrifice for his own sins and the sins of the people.

Thank God that He sent Jesus to be the Sacrifice for our sins. When John the Baptist saw Jesus, he said, "Behold the Lamb of God, which taketh away the sin of the world." (John 1:29)

Jesus, the only sinless, spotless Lamb, became the perfect sacrifice for your sins. Not only that, He became your High Priest, the mediator between you and God.

"Seeing then that we have a great high priest, that is passed into the heavens, Jesus, the Son of God, let us hold fast our profession. For we have not a high priest which cannot be touched with the feeling of our infirmities; but was in all points tempted like as we are, yet without sin." (Hebrews 4:14,15)

Since Jesus lived here in the flesh, He knows what it's like to be tempted to sin. Yet He never gave into temptation. Now He prays for you to overcome temptation.

"Wherefore he is able also to save them to the uttermost that come unto God by him, seeing he ever liveth to make intercession for them. For such a high priest became us, who is holy, harmless, undefiled, separate from sinners, and made higher than the heavens; who needeth not daily, as those high priests, to offer up sacrifice first for his own sins, and then for the people's; for this he did once, when he offered up himself [on the cross]." *(Hebrews 7:25-27)*

When Jesus died on the cross for your sins, He said, "It is finished." You no longer need to offer sacrifices for your sin. He is your High Priest. How wonderful He is! Receive His gift of salvation. He loves you so much!

Say, "Thank You, Jesus, for being the perfect sacrifice for my sins. You are my High Priest."

46

I Think Good Thoughts

Being health conscious, I try to eat nutritious food. One day the Lord said to me, "What you think is as important as what you eat."

Toxic thoughts can cause toxicity in the body too. Even the health of your bones is reliant on your thoughts, whether joyful or sad.

"A merry heart doeth good like a medicine, but a broken spirit drieth the bones." (Proverbs 17:22)

There is a battle for your mind. The devil attacks with thoughts of fear, worry, condemnation, inferiority, depression, temptation, and negativity. The enemy tries to control us with thoughts. You must win the battle for your mind! Be aware of what you are thinking. Ask yourself, where is this thought coming from? You have the power to choose what you allow into your thought life. If it's not good, kick it out! God will help.

"For the weapons of our warfare are not carnal, but mighty through God, to the pulling down of strongholds; casting down imaginations, and every high thing that exalteth itself against the knowledge of God, and bringing into captivity every thought to the obedience of Christ." (2 Corinthians 10:4,5)

Thoughts affect emotions, words, health, and actions. Cast down negative imaginations. To stop harassing thoughts, choose to focus on God's positive promises and speak them aloud. Listen to the Bible online. Play worship music and sing!

Thinking gloomy thoughts makes one sad. Feeling down can steal motivation, energy and weaken the immune system. Joy gives strength and stamina.

"...for the joy of the Lord is your strength." (Nehemiah 8:10b)

Whatever we think about is what we become.

"For as he thinketh in his heart, so is he..." (Proverbs 23:7a)

That's why you need to know what God says about you and think on that.

Are you forgetful? Don't say, "I can't remember." Say, "It will come to me." When I catch myself saying, "I forgot," I immediately change it to, "I just remembered." Say, "I have perfect recall. I remember names instantly." This really helps.

It's easy to let your mind wander. Then thoughts can spiral down into negative thinking. Instead of having private thoughts, talk to God about everything throughout your day. Have God in all your thoughts.

Philippians 4:8 says to think about things that are true, honest, just, pure, lovely, and of good report. What puts a smile on your face? It could be a child's giggle, a beautiful sunset, the aroma of your Grandma's ginger cake. Think about those things.

The Bible states to love the Lord with all your mind. When you keep your mind fixed on the Lord, you will have perfect peace. Meditate on (mull over in your mind) the Word of God. Worry is meditating on bad stuff. Think about God instead.

Say, "I cast down imaginations, and bring every thought captive to the obedience of Christ."

47

I Share the Good News of the Gospel

A notice came to our house on Fire Prevention, providing a checklist of preparation in case of a fire. As I read, I wondered how many people have actually prepared, by installing smoke alarms, cleaning dryer vents, and creating an escape plan. The difference could mean life or death.

Death. How many have prepared for that? Not only with Life Insurance, but preparing for life after death. Many people don't want to think about death, so they avoid the subject. Yet, what is decided here and now will determine the outcome for eternity. It's imperative to prepare now.

Forever is a long, long time.

If you saw a house on fire, you would warn the people inside.

"Wake up! Get out!"

You would readily alert them of danger in order to save their lives. That is what you must do for people who don't know Jesus. It's urgent!

Jesus said, "Go ye into all the world and preach the gospel to every creature." (Mark 16:15)

What are we to say? Tell them:

"Heaven is a beautiful place which God has made. The streets are made of gold, and the gates of pearl. There will be no crying, death or sickness there. It is pure and holy. But how can we get there? We are not pure and holy. That's called sin and it separates us from God. The good news is that God loves us so much that He gave His only Son, Jesus, to take the punishment for our sin. Believe and confess that Jesus died for your sin, and rose from the dead. Repent and turn from sin, receive Jesus as your personal Lord, your new boss. The blood of Jesus washes away all your sin, making you pure and holy. Now you have a fresh start. By reading the Bible, talking to God and spending time with other believers, you will grow in the Lord."

Lead them in a prayer to receive Jesus. (You may use the one on Page 143.)

Tell others how you came to the Lord. Your testimony is powerful.

Jesus said, "I am the way, the truth, and the life. No man cometh unto the Father, but by me." (John 14:6)

The gospel is good news. Share it with enthusiasm!

"He that winneth souls is wise." (Proverbs 11:30b)

There is much joy in leading someone to the Lord. Try it. You will be blessed.

Say, "I will go into all the world (my community, workplace, peer group) and preach the gospel (good news) of Jesus."

48

I Stay Humble

Isn't it awful to watch a show-off? Someone who is pretending to be better than they are, putting on airs, trying to show up everyone else. It's not a pretty sight. In an attempt to get others' approval, they actually turn people off. Someone who is proud does not fully understand who they are in Christ.

When you humble yourself and give God all the glory for your abilities, then God can promote you. Pride is a lie, after all, for what can you do apart from the One Who keeps your heart beating? Jesus said that without Him you can do nothing. But, with Him, you can do all things.

Pride is a nasty trap and can sneak up on you. You may not see it. Ask God to show you if there is any pride in your heart, so you can get rid of it.

The Lord hates a proud look. Everyone who is proud in heart is an abomination to God.

"Pride goeth before destruction, and a haughty spirit before a fall." (Proverbs 16:18)

Pride is a person's downfall but a humble person is blessed.

"By humility and the fear of the Lord are riches, and honour, and life." (Proverbs 22:4)

"He hath showed thee, O man, what is good; and what doth the Lord require of thee, but to do justly, and to love mercy, and to walk humbly with thy God." (Micah 6:8)

114

"...be clothed with humility: for God resisteth the proud, and giveth grace to the humble. Humble yourselves therefore under the mighty hand of God, that he may exalt you in due time."
(1 Peter 5:5b,6)

Even Jesus humbled Himself while on the earth, although He is King of kings!

"Let this mind be in you, which was also in Christ Jesus: who, being in the form of God, thought it not robbery to be equal with God; but made himself of no reputation, and took upon him the form of a servant, and was made in the likeness of men: and being found in fashion as a man, he humbled himself, and became obedient unto death, even the death of the cross. Wherefore God also hath highly exalted him, and given him a name which is above every name." (Philippians 2:5-9)

One day every knee will bow to Jesus and every tongue will confess that Jesus Christ is Lord!

Say, "I humble myself before God, and He will lift me up."

49

I Am Treasured

The Lord wants family. Just as parents want the best for their children, so does God. How gratifying it is for a parent to see their child obedient, loving, and joyful. The Lord desires this for His kids also. He takes notice of those who are.

"Then they that feared the Lord spake often one to another: and the Lord hearkened, and heard it, and a book of remembrance was written before him for them that feared the Lord, and that thought upon his name. And they shall be mine, saith the Lord of hosts, in that day when I make up my jewels; and I will spare them, as a man spareth his own son that serveth him." (Malachi 3:16,17)

The Lord declared over His people, the children of Israel, "Now therefore, if ye will obey my voice indeed, and keep my covenant, then ye shall be a peculiar [special] treasure unto me above all people: for all the earth is mine." (Exodus 19:5)

"Keep me as the apple of the eye; hide me under the shadow of thy wings." (Psalm 17:8)

The Lord watches over you day and night. You are precious to Him. He thinks you are special. He sees all of your hard work, hears your prayers and praise, and acknowledges your love and service for others. He is keeping records. He wants to bless you here and also reward you in eternity.

Jesus said, "And behold, I come quickly; and my reward is with me, to give every man according as his work shall be." (Revelation 22:12)

I think we will be amazed at what God has in store for us. Now is the time to work and be faithful—to live for Him; then we can enjoy Him forever.

Say, "God treasures me and will reward me one day."

50

I Wait Upon the Lord

It's hard to wait. When trials come and you need answers, you want God to act *now*. Yet there is great benefit in waiting on the Lord. As you pray and believe God for an answer in the waiting room of life, it may seem like He is not doing anything. The enemy may tell you that God doesn't care and isn't going to answer your prayers. Remember the devil is a liar. While you wait, God is working behind the scenes. So when you pray, believe you will receive. Pray God's Word. When we pray what God says, we are praying His will. Take God at His Word, for He keeps His promises.

"But they that wait upon the Lord shall renew their strength; they shall mount up with wings as eagles; they shall run, and not be weary; and they shall walk, and not faint." (Isaiah 40:31)

When you pray, expect God to answer!

"Truly my soul waiteth upon God: from him cometh my salvation." (Psalm 62:1)

"My soul, wait thou only upon God; for my expectation is from him." (Psalm 62:5)

Keep seeking God. Don't panic. You may think you need something right away, yet God knows the right timing and what is best for you. He is your loving Father. Trust Him. He sees the bigger picture. Thank Him that He is working.

"Wait on the Lord: be of good courage, and he shall strengthen thine heart: wait, I say, on the Lord." (Psalm 27:14)

Waiting on the Lord is also a great way to get to know Him better. Seek His face. Enjoy Him. Don't only call upon Him when in crisis. Get into the habit of spending daily time with Him. Let Him do a work in your heart.

Maybe He is waiting on you.

Say, "I wait on the Lord. I know He hears me and He is working."

51

I Sleep Well

Sleep is important for health, good attitude, concentration and stamina. Yet stress, hormones, busyness, and worry can cause insomnia.

I need to unwind before going to bed. I can't just stop, hit the pillow, and fall asleep. My husband can. He tells me to reach up and turn off the switch in my brain, and everything will go dark. "I don't have a switch!" I reply. My mind won't go into a nothing box; I have to think about something. So, before I retire, I spend time with the Lord, write in my journal and read a bit. Getting my thoughts sorted out first helps me relax and fall asleep.

"When thou liest down, thou shalt not be afraid: yea, thou shalt lie down, and thy sleep shall be sweet." (Proverbs 3:24)

*Practical things to get sleepy are: eat a banana, drink warm milk, relax in the tub, take some magnesium and Vitamin D to relax your muscles. Tart cherry juice is a natural source of melatonin, needed for sleep. Take 1/4 to 1/2 cup an hour before bed. Avoid the computer screen just before bed, or use the night eye protection mode. Do your bedtime routine early, then read until you feel sleepy. Put on some peaceful music. Fighting insomnia won't help you relax. Instead think, *Okay, I'm not sleeping, but I'm resting.* Next thing you know, it's morning!

Norman Vincent Peale's tailor told him to empty the pockets of his suit jacket before he went to bed, so the pockets wouldn't lose shape. Similarly, empty your mind of all cares before you climb into bed, or the cares will get into bed with you! Give them all to God; thank Him that He is handling them. Then go to sleep.

Control racing thoughts with God's Word. Think of verses from A-Z. For example, "**A**sk and it shall be given you. **B**elieve on the Lord Jesus Christ, and thou shalt be saved. **C**asting all your care upon him, for he careth for you." For anxious thoughts, meditate on verses about peace. This is another great reason to memorize Scripture!

If sleep delays, don't waste time. Pray. When my Aunt Margaret, age 95, can't sleep, she prays for her whole family by name and situation. It takes her two hours. As well, God has given her over 100 poems in the night. "I don't just lie there!" she laughs.

If I'm getting to bed late, but need to get up early, I ask God to give me a good, quality sleep, regardless of the quantity of sleep, and help me wake up refreshed. He does.

"He [the Lord] will not suffer thy foot to be moved: he that keepeth thee will not slumber. Behold, he that keepeth Israel shall neither slumber nor sleep. The Lord is thy keeper..." (Psalm 121:3,4,5a)

The Lord doesn't sleep. While you sleep, God is awake and taking care of you.

"I will both lay me down in peace, and sleep: for thou, Lord, only makest me dwell in safety." (Psalm 4:8)

Say, "The Lord gives His beloved sleep." (Psalm 127:2b)

*Disclaimer: This is not medical advice, only suggestions. If you have sleep problems, contact your health practitioner.

52

I Am Blessed

When God created the earth and put man and woman in the garden of Eden, He blessed them. Everything was beautiful, brand new, and amazing. God said it was good. When Adam and Eve sinned, they lost the blessing and mankind came under a curse. But Jesus Christ took the curse for us on the cross.

"Christ hath redeemed us from the curse of the law, being made a curse for us: for it is written, Cursed is every one that hangeth on a tree. That the blessing of Abraham might come on the Gentiles through Jesus Christ; that we might receive the promise of the Spirit through faith. And if ye be Christ's, then are ye Abraham's seed, and heirs according to the promise." (Galatians 3:13,14,29)

Now the Lord had said unto Abram, "Get thee out of thy country...and I will make of thee a great nation, and I will bless thee, and make thy name great; and thou shalt be a blessing." (Genesis 12:1,2)

Blessing means special favour, mercy, benefit, approval, or a gift bestowed by God.

God blessed Abraham. He was very rich. If you are in Christ, those blessings are yours too. You are blessed with the blessings of Abraham.

"Even as Abraham believed God, and it was accounted to him for righteousness. Know ye therefore that they which are of faith, the same are the children of Abraham. And the scripture, foreseeing that God would justify the heathen through faith,

preached before the gospel unto Abraham, saying, In thee shall all nations be blessed. So then they which be of faith are blessed with faithful Abraham." (Galatians 3:6-9)

Abraham was a man of faith. He believed what God said about him (that he would have a child in his old age), and it happened. His faith and obedience entitled him to the blessings of God.

"Blessed be the Lord who daily loadeth us with benefits, even the God of our salvation." (Psalm 68:19)

"The blessing of the Lord, it maketh rich and he addeth no sorrow with it." (Proverbs 10:22)

"He will bless them that fear the Lord, both small and great. Ye are blessed of the Lord which made heaven and earth." (Psalm 115:13,15)

God is constantly pouring out His blessings on you. Thank Him for all the blessings He gives you here, and for all of eternity. We are blessed to be a blessing to others.

Say, "I am blessed of the Lord Who made heaven and earth."

53

I Am Strong in the Lord

Is your battle long and hard? Do you lack the strength to go on? There is hope. God is there to give you strength. Whether you need physical or emotional strength, reach out to Him.

Speak out and meditate on the following verses.

"...Be strong in the Lord, and in the power of his might." (Ephesians 6:10)

"I can do all things through Christ which strengtheneth me." *(Philippians 4:13)*

"In God is my salvation and my glory: the rock of my strength, and my refuge, is in God." (Psalm 62:7)

"I will go in the strength of the Lord God." (Psalm 71:16a)

"O Lord of hosts, my King, and my God...Blessed is the man whose strength is in thee..." (Psalm 84:3b, 5a)

"The Lord is my strength and song, and is become my salvation." (Psalm 118:14)

"I will love thee, O Lord, my strength. The Lord is my rock, and my fortress, and my deliverer; my God, my strength, in whom I will trust; my buckler, and the horn of my salvation, and my high tower." (Psalm 18:1,2)

"But the God of all grace, who hath called us unto his eternal glory by Christ Jesus, after that ye have suffered a while, make you perfect, establish, strengthen [and] settle you." (1 Peter 5:10)

"He giveth power to the faint; and to them that have no might he increaseth strength." (Isaiah 40:29)

"...for the joy of the Lord is your strength." (Nehemiah 8:10b)

When you begin to focus on God, not problems, thinking of how majestic He is, how kind and loving, it will fill you with joy. The joy of the Lord *is* your strength. Feeling downcast saps your strength. So look to God. He can do anything. Think about Him, talk to Him, and let Him strengthen you.

Even if you feel weak, you can declare, "Let the weak say, I am strong." (Joel 3:10b)

Say, "I am strong in the Lord, and in the power of His might."

54

I Live Holy

God wants you to be holy, for He is holy. Jesus is coming back for a pure, spotless bride—those who have received Him as their Saviour and made Him Lord of their lives. Allow Him to be your Manager.

When you become a Christian, you are made new. But sometimes there are habits or activities that need to change. It's the process of becoming holy, yielding daily to God's Holy Spirit in you, immersing yourself in God's manual for life, the Bible, and refusing to live by your flesh. The flesh is mindless; it wants what it wants, regardless of consequence. Your born again spirit must rule over your flesh. You cannot continue to live in willful sin.

"For God hath not called us unto uncleanness, but unto holiness." (1 Thessalonians 4:7)

God is looking for purity in the people who make up His Church.

"...Even as Christ also loved the church, and gave himself for it; that he might sanctify and cleanse it with the washing of water by the word, that he might present it to himself a glorious church, not having spot, or wrinkle, or any such thing; but that it should be holy and without blemish." (Ephesians 5:25-27)

Being born again, living holy and holding nothing against anyone is the only way we will see God.

"Follow peace with all men, and holiness, without which no man shall see the Lord." (Hebrews 12:14)

Examine your life. Think about your personal pursuits, your reading material, the content of your TV, cell phone and computer programs. Would Jesus join you in these activities?

Remember His *Holy* Spirit resides in you. Wherever you go, He goes. Yield to Him. The Bible says do not quench or grieve the Holy Spirit.

If there are any pursuits, even in your thought life, that need to be cleaned up, confess it to God and ask Him to help you get free from all sins and addictions. He will give you the power to break every chain of bondage, as you yield to Him. Use your sword, the Word of God, to speak over the sin. It may be a battle at first, but continue until you get complete victory!

Yield to the Holy Spirit daily, and let Him change you.

Say, "I can live holy by yielding to the Holy Spirit's power."

55

I Can Hear God's Voice

When Samuel was a young boy, he served the Lord with Eli, the priest. One night, when Samuel was in bed, he heard his name, "Samuel! Samuel!" He got up and ran into Eli's room. "Here I am. You called me?" Eli said he didn't call him and sent him back to bed. A second time Samuel heard his name and ran to Eli. Again he was sent back to bed. The third time Eli realized it was the Lord calling Samuel. Eli told Samuel to go lie down, and when he hears the voice calling him again, he should say, "Speak, Lord, for thy servant heareth." This time the Lord spoke a message to Samuel. See 1 Samuel 3: 1-10.

God wants to talk to you too. The key is to listen for Him and recognize His voice.

Jesus said, "I am the good shepherd: the good shepherd giveth his life for the sheep. My sheep hear my voice, and I know them, and they follow me." (John 10:11,27)

A shepherd stays with his sheep, protects them, leads them, and talks to them. They know his voice, but they will not follow a stranger. How well do you know the Good Shepherd? Do you hear His voice? You can't hear Him as easily if you are rushing about, distracted. Give Him your time. Sit in His presence. Worship Him. Then get quiet.

"Be still, and know that I am God." (Psalm 46:10a)

Prayer is a two-way conversation. When you talk to someone, you both have something to say. You speak and you listen. So it is with God.

God speaks through the Bible. He also speaks by His Spirit. Ask Him to speak to you. Open your Bible. Have a pen and journal handy. As you spend time with Him daily, you will learn to recognize His voice. Probably not an audible voice, but words from His Spirit to yours, like a flow of thoughts. Write it down. The Bible states that when you pray, God hears and will answer.

He can give you specific instructions. One day He told me to go and visit a lady and give her a certain tract, a booklet about salvation. I did. She prayed and accepted Jesus as her Lord!

After developing the habit of hearing God's voice, I have filled many journals over the years with messages from Him. Sometimes He gives a word of encouragement, sometimes a rebuke. He often gives direction and solutions. He knows what you are going through and is there to help. It's wonderful to have close fellowship with Him.

When you begin hearing from the Lord, and journal His words, you might want to have a mature Christ follower read it over. It will never contradict God's written Word. Learn to listen to the Lord throughout the day. He wants to speak to you all the time. You need to stay tuned into His frequency so you can hear Him. God wants to encourage and direct you, and also fellowship with you.

Say, "When I listen, I can hear God's voice."

56

I Acknowledge God in Everything

Should you pray about trivial matters? Surely God isn't interested in a sick kitty or finding misplaced keys. Yes, He is! He is interested in what concerns you, because He loves you.

After working in a full-time position for eleven years, I wanted a change. I began to ask the Lord where He wanted me. I kept running across the same passage in Isaiah 29, verses 11 and 12. "And the vision of all is become unto you as the words of a book that is sealed, which men deliver to one that is learned, saying, 'Read this, I pray thee,' and he saith, 'I cannot, for it is sealed.' And the book is delivered to him that is not learned, saying, 'Read this, I pray thee,' and he saith, 'I am not learned.'"

I wondered what this could mean. At the time, I hadn't learned to hear God's voice, but I knew He was speaking to me through His Word. Although the Word of God was written centuries ago, it is living and powerful. (See Hebrews 4:12) That makes it relevant, so it still speaks to us today.

I knew I was to leave my job, but I was afraid to tell my boss! He was like an army general and I found him very intimidating. One day, I was sitting at the lake during lunch hour, praying about it. God took me to Isaiah 51:12,13a.

"I, even I, am he that comforteth you; who art thou, that thou shouldest be afraid of a man who shall die...and forgettest the Lord thy maker?"

That did it. I went right back to the office and summoned the manager. He came right away (which was a small miracle in itself) and I told him I was leaving. It was easy!

Oh, and the verses about reading? An employment opportunity opened up at a local Literacy Council. I applied and got the job. For the next three years, I enjoyed working in the office, as well as tutoring adults in reading. I even helped one lady who wanted to read her Bible. In the first session, she accepted Jesus as her Lord!

Sometimes we think we know best, when God has a better way. That's why we need to acknowledge Him in everything.

"Trust in the Lord with all thine heart; and lean not unto thine own understanding. In all thy ways acknowledge him and he shall direct thy paths." (Proverbs 3:5,6)

Say, "I acknowledge God in everything and let Him direct me."

57

I Seek God's Face

One morning, at the breakfast table, I asked my young daughter, "Did you know you can play hide and seek with God?"

"Wouldn't that be something," she replied.

I told her to ask God where to read in the Bible and then open it up. Since her Bible wasn't handy, she reached across the table to use her dad's Bible. When she opened it, she found a note her dad had written to her months before. It read, "Ha, ha, ha. I found you!"

Isn't God fun?

"And ye shall seek me, and find me, when ye shall search for me with all your heart. And I will be found of you, saith the Lord." (Jeremiah 29:13,14a)

"That they should seek the Lord, if haply they might feel after him, and find him, though he be not far from every one of us: For in him we live, and move, and have our being; as certain also of your own poets have said, For we are also His offspring." (Acts 17:27,28)

Author Tommy Tenney tells of playing hide and seek with his toddler. He would hide, but expose the toe of his shoe. After all, he wanted her to find him! When she discovered him they would laugh and rejoice together. God wants to be found too. He wants to know if we really want to find Him. Are you willing to search for Him?

Seek the Lord Himself. Seek to get to know Him better. Study His attributes. Know what pleases Him. (Faith pleases Him; also obedience, and singing to Him) Don't simply seek His hands (for your needs and blessings) but seek His face, His presence, His character. When you draw close to God, He will draw near to you. See James 4:8a.

"When thou saidst, Seek ye my face; my heart said unto thee, Thy face, Lord, will I seek." (Psalm 27:8)

Say, "I will seek the Lord daily."

58

I Claim God's Promises For

My Children

There are many promises in the Bible to claim for your children. Ask God to show you Scriptures to hold onto and speak over your children and grandchildren. He wants to help you. God wants to partner with you to raise your children. Ask the Holy Spirit for His wisdom and direction for each situation.

"[The Lord God] shall gently lead those that are with young." (Isaiah 40:11b)

"...I will pour my spirit upon thy seed, and my blessing upon thine offspring." (Isaiah 44:3b)

"And all thy children shall be taught of the Lord; and great shall be the peace of thy children." (Isaiah 54:13)

"Though hand join in hand, the wicked shall not be unpunished: but the seed of the righteous shall be delivered." (Proverbs 11:21)

"Lo, children are an heritage of the Lord: and the fruit of the womb is his reward." (Psalm 127:3)

"He maketh the barren woman to keep house, and to be a joyful mother of children. Praise ye the Lord." (Psalm 113:9)

"Yea, thou shalt see thy children's children..." (Psalm 128:6)

"The Lord shall increase you more and more, you and your children." (Psalm 115:14)

"...but as for me and my house, we will serve the Lord." (Joshua 24:15b)

There are many more Scriptures to pray over your children. Teach your children from the Bible. Talk about the Lord when in the car, at home, and outdoors. Let them see you reading your Bible, singing to the King, running to God when troubles come, and rejoicing when God answers. Pray with them. Daily bless them before they leave the house. Claim God's promises over them. Teach them they can talk to God about anything, anytime, anywhere. Let them know God is real and is there for them.

Perhaps you have a prodigal. You can stand on and speak Jeremiah 31:16,17:

"Thus saith the Lord; Refrain thy voice from weeping, and thine eyes from tears: for thy work shall be rewarded, saith the Lord; and they shall come again from the land of the enemy. And there is hope in thine end, saith the Lord, that thy children shall come again to their own border."

Say, "My children are blessed of the Lord."

59

I'm a Doer of the Word

Knowing I need to exercise, I bought a fitness DVD. It had great exercises. I totally enjoyed them...while sitting at the table eating lunch. Did those exercises benefit me in any way? Hardly! I didn't do them.

In order to know what God wants you to do, you need to read the Bible and listen to messages. But, you can't just be a hearer of God's Word. You need to do what it says.

James 1:22-25 says, "But be ye doers of the word, and not hearers only, deceiving your own selves. For if any be a hearer of the word, and not a doer, he is like unto a man beholding his natural face in a glass: for he beholdeth himself, and goeth his way, and straightway forgetteth what manner of man he was. But whoso looketh into the perfect law of liberty, and continueth therein, he being not a forgetful hearer, but a doer of the work, this man shall be blessed in his deed."

Jesus said, "Ye are my friends, if ye **do** whatsoever I command you. Henceforth I call you not servants; for the servant knoweth not what his lord doeth: but I have called you friends; for all things that I have heard of my Father I have made known unto you." (John 15:14,15)

"...Abraham believed God, and it was imputed unto him for righteousness and he was called the Friend of God." (James 2:23b) Abraham obeyed God by believing what God said.

A mother asks her teenager to take the trash out, and the teen responds, "Sure, Mom. I love you." If the youth doesn't take out the trash, and just continues playing video games, where is the love? It's just lip-service.

You don't want to be like the person Jesus described, who calls Him Lord, but does not obey Him.

*"Not every one that saith unto me, Lord, Lord, shall enter into the kingdom of heaven; but he that **doeth** the will of my Father which is in heaven." (Matthew 7:21)*

It's not enough to say, "I love Jesus." You need to show your love by doing what He says.

Say, "I do what the Lord says."

60

I Eagerly Watch For Jesus' Return

Jesus is coming back soon. Before He went home to heaven, He said to look at world events that would usher in His return. It will be like the days of Noah. Sin abounded. People were doing their own thing, oblivious to God and His ways. It was business as usual when, suddenly, the flood came and it was too late. Similarly, Jesus will come suddenly, without warning. He told us to *watch*.

"Watch therefore: for ye know not what hour your Lord doth come. Therefore be ye also ready: for in such an hour as ye think not the Son of man cometh." (Matthew 24:42,44)

"For yourselves know perfectly that the day of the Lord so cometh as a thief in the night." (1 Thessalonians 5:2)

"Looking for that blessed hope, and the glorious appearing of the great God and our Saviour Jesus Christ; Who gave himself for us, that he might redeem us from all iniquity, and purify unto himself a peculiar people, zealous of good works." (Titus 2:13,14)

"And to wait for his Son from heaven, whom he raised from the dead, even Jesus, which delivered us from the wrath to come." (1 Thessalonians 1:10)

"For if we believe that Jesus died and rose again, even so them also which sleep in Jesus [Christians who died] will God bring with him. For this we say unto you by the word of the Lord, that we which are alive and remain unto the coming of the

Lord shall not prevent them which are asleep. For the Lord himself shall descend from heaven with a shout, with the voice of the archangel, and with the trump of God: and the dead in Christ shall rise first: then we which are alive and remain shall be caught up together with them in the clouds, to meet the Lord in the air: and so shall we ever be with the Lord."
(1 Thessalonians 4:14-17)

"...When the Son of man cometh shall he find faith on the earth?" (Luke 18:8b)

"He which testifieth these things saith, Surely I come quickly. Amen. Even so, come, Lord Jesus." (Revelation 22:20)

"And the very God of peace sanctify you wholly; and I pray God your whole spirit and soul and body be preserved blameless unto the coming of our Lord Jesus Christ."
(1 Thessalonians 5:23)

Watch. Be ready. Tell others. Live godly.
He's coming!

Say, "I will tell others about Jesus and get ready for His return."

SUMMARY

Divine Downloads will make a positive difference in your life when you *believe* and *speak* these truths. Be aware of your words. Practise speaking and praying the promises of God from His Word. You will see the fruit, for God keeps His promises.

A good example of this is Abraham, a childless senior who believed God when he heard that he and his wife would have a child in their old age! Abraham didn't go by what it looked like in the natural, what other people said, or how he felt. He said what God said, and believed God's word above everything else. He mixed his faith and his words with God's words and received the promise!

"And he [God] brought him [Abram] forth abroad, and said, Look now toward heaven, and tell the stars, if thou be able to number them: and he said unto him, So shall thy seed be. And he believed in the Lord; and he counted it to him for righteousness." (Genesis 15:5,6)

"...the faith of Abraham; who is the father of us all, (as it is written, I have made thee a father of many nations,) before him whom he believed, even God, who quickeneth [makes alive] the dead, and *calleth those things which be not as though they were.* Who against hope believed in hope, that he might become the father of many nations, according to that which was spoken, so shall thy seed be. And being not weak in faith, he considered not his own body now dead, when he was about a hundred years old, neither yet the deadness of Sarah's womb: he staggered not at the promise of God through unbelief; but was strong in faith, giving glory to God; and being fully persuaded that, what he had promised he was also able to perform." (Romans 4:16b-21)

God did keep His promise. Sarah gave birth to Isaac, which means laughter. Wouldn't you laugh if God gave you a baby when you were ninety years old?

Don't say, "It is what it is." No! God can change things, even if it looks impossible. Call those things that are not as though they are. If God's Word says so, you say so. Get hold of this truth in your heart and it will change your situation. No matter what you are going through, what it looks like, or how you feel, give God's Word the final authority in your life. Say what God says about you! Watch God's powerful, living Word change things, and even change you!

Say, "Let the words of my mouth, and the meditation of my heart, be acceptable in thy sight, O Lord, my strength, and my redeemer." (Psalm 19:14)

Would you like to know Jesus personally?

Do you want a 24/7 friend? Jesus loves you very much. He has good plans for you. However, there is a problem. It's called sin. The Bible says we've all sinned. No sin or evil can enter heaven. God is perfect, holy and just. Sin has to be punished, just as someone who breaks the law has to pay for the crime. God knew we could never do enough good works to pay for our sins. That's why He sent His own Son, Jesus, Who never sinned, to take our place. Jesus died on the cross to take the punishment we deserve. Then Jesus rose again from the dead and went back to heaven, to prepare a place for all who have received Him personally and who live for Him.

If you would like to receive God's free gift of salvation, you can do it now. Here's how:

Admit you are a sinner. We have all sinned, whether thinking bad thoughts, telling a lie, stealing, or rebelling against God. No one is as holy as God.

"For all have sinned, and come short of the glory of God." (Romans 3:23)

"For the wages of sin is death; but the gift of God is eternal life through Jesus Christ our Lord." (Romans 6:23)

Sin has consequences. Jesus came to save sinners.

Believe in your heart that Jesus died on the cross to take the punishment for your sins, and He rose again from the dead.

Confess aloud that you believe Jesus died for your sins. Tell someone.

"That if thou shalt confess with your mouth the Lord Jesus, and shalt believe in thine heart that God hath raised Him from the dead, thou shalt be saved." (Romans 10:9)

"If we confess our sins, he is faithful and just to forgive us our sins, and to cleanse us from all unrighteousness." (1 John 1:9)

Repent (turn away from sin) and ask God to forgive your sins.

"...Repent, and be baptized every one of you in the name of Jesus Christ for the remission of sins, and ye shall receive the gift of the Holy Ghost." (Acts 2:38)

Receive Jesus as your Saviour and make Him your Lord (Boss, Life Coach, Mentor).

"But as many as received him, to them gave he power to become the sons of God, even to them that believe on His name." (John 1:12)

Ask Him to fill you with His Holy Spirit, Who will give you the power to live for God.

Pray: Heavenly Father, I know I'm a sinner. I'm sorry. Please forgive me. I want to turn from my sin. I believe You gave Your Son, Jesus, Who died on the cross to take the punishment for my sin. He rose from the dead. I now ask Jesus to be my Saviour and Lord. Come into my life and take over. Fill me with Your Holy Spirit and give me the power to live for You. In Jesus' name I pray. Amen.

Congratulations! You are now a child of God. Tell someone that you received Christ. Next, you need to grow. Read the Bible and talk to God daily. Ask Him to direct you to a good church. Get to know the One Who loves you and gave His life for you. Ask Him for His plan for your life. You have just begun a great adventure!

Made in the USA
Lexington, KY
12 November 2019

56915824R00090